LEAVE IT ALL

The Journal of a Maybe Missionary

chelsea greenwood

Inspira
LITERARY SOLUTIONS

Leave It All: The Journal of a Maybe Missionary
First Edition, 2019
Copyright © 2019 by Chelsea Greenwood

ISBN: 978-1-7332679-0-8

To order additional books:
www.chelseathewriter.com
www.amazon.com

Editorial and Book Packaging: Inspira Literary Solutions, Gig Harbor, WA
Book Cover Design, Interior Maps, and Layout: Brianna Showalter, Ruston, WA
Printed in the USA by Ingram Spark

For C Squad:
Aly, Alyssa, Andrea, Arden, Belle, Beka, Beth,
Bobby, Bre, CC, Caitlin, Carly, Cody, Courtney, Daniel,
Deborah, Dillon, Heather, Heidi, Hope, Jacob, Jason,
Jayce, Jeff, Jinnae, Kelly, Kelsey, Kim, Kori, Lacey,
Laura, Margaret, Mateo, Michelle, Miranda, Nate,
Nicole, Rita, Robyn, Shannon, Sharon, Stacie,
Stephanie, Tara, Tony, and Wendy.

Contents

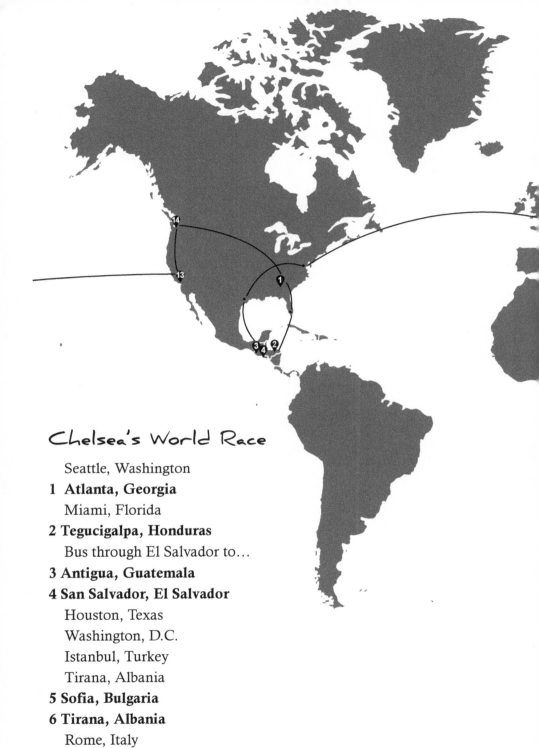

Chelsea's World Race

Seattle, Washington
1 **Atlanta, Georgia**
   Miami, Florida
2 **Tegucigalpa, Honduras**
   Bus through El Salvador to…
3 **Antigua, Guatemala**
4 **San Salvador, El Salvador**
   Houston, Texas
   Washington, D.C.
   Istanbul, Turkey
   Tirana, Albania
5 **Sofia, Bulgaria**
6 **Tirana, Albania**
   Rome, Italy
   Addis Ababa, Ethiopia
   Harare, Zimbabwe

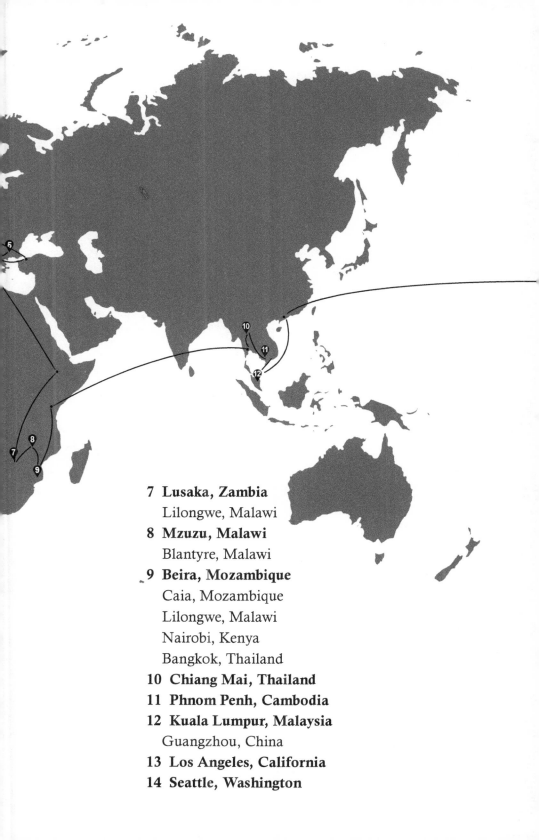

PREFACE

On January 9, 2014, 41 North American adults known collectively as C Squad, Third Generation, began an 11-month, 11-country, interdenominational Christian mission trip called the World Race. I was one of them.

I was a 23-year-old woman from the South Puget Sound, and had just graduated from Vassar College in Poughkeepsie, New York. My time in New York had entailed four years of clinging to my earnest, lifelong Christian faith while earning a bachelor's degree in world religions in the musty bowels of what The Princeton Review then deemed the "nation's most secular campus." By my last semester, I was burned out from the struggle, and doubting that God even *existed*.

That's when God called me to be a missionary.

So, in the hope of curing my skepticism, the joy of following Jesus, and the thrill of backpacking around the world (and returning home a sexy, tan goddess), I signed up to serve in 11 countries in 11 months on the World Race.

This book is a distillation of the journals, blogs, and emails I produced about the World Race between 2011 and 2018. Some conversations are recounted from memory and therefore approximate, and a few names and identifying details have been altered to protect characters' anonymity. Some blog entries have been altered from my original World Race blog. Everything described is true as I remember it, and I have tried to leave it all: the miraculous bits, the funny bits, the ignorant bits, the shit bits, the cynical bits, and the faithful bits.

If I regret anything about this, it's that I have written too much about myself and not nearly enough about C Squad, my 40 wild companions with whom I circumnavigated the world. I've done my best to chisel my journals into something beautiful and stubbornly true to the events and attitudes of 2014, but the grand scale of the World Race and my own self-centeredness have necessitated the exclusion of inside jokes, conversations, and struggles that were integral to the experiences of my companions. But know that in the list of people who made this book worth writing, my C Squad family is first and foremost.

I also want to thank my parents and siblings for their decades of love and support. Thanks to Joseph, Michelle, Chris, Jacob, Kat, Kassi, and Grace, for reading my unfinished manuscript and giving me their best, brutal feedback. Dennis, Arlyn, Heather, Kerry, Tim, and Brianna, thank you for introducing me to publishing and for making this book real. Thanks to Tony, who let me write so much about him.

Finally, thank you to every single person who has told me to keep writing, whether it's been in a comment on my blog, a surprise text, or a casual "So, when is that book coming out?" It is profoundly—almost dangerously—encouraging to hear, over and over, that the thing you love to do is the thing you must do.

BEFORE

Two and a half years before the World Race

I'm flipping through an article in a magazine I found on the coffee table and I am struck by a photo of people crossing a river, carrying backpacks over their heads. It looks like a gritty, glorious adventure. The article is about the World Race: a mission trip to 11 countries in 11 months. The World Race is now on my mind.

One year before the World Race

It is January 2013 and I am crying into an airplane window. I am flying home from a conference on global missions in St. Louis. I arrived skeptical and I'm leaving ruined and resolved because I made a choice.

I'm going to apply to the World Race. I'm going to be a missionary and leave everything I know to travel to 11 countries in 11 months and serve God and see the world. I am so afraid of this choice, yet I am so overjoyed at this choice.

I'm from a white, middle class family of conservative, earnest Christians in the Pacific Northwest. I've had this faith longer than I can remember. I know all about Jesus. I love Jesus. I want others to love Jesus. I want others to know that Jesus loves them.

But I also have a brain that works against my faith. I'm finishing a college degree in world religions, and the older I get, the more doubts I have that my faith is in anything real, so how is it that I am now smashing my face into a window, weeping in determination to proclaim Christ to the world?

At the conference, I heard a lot about following Jesus, no matter what it costs or where it takes us. I heard stories of martyrs who lost their lives because they believed so hard in the Gospel, they were killed. I heard speakers detail their grimy, joyous lives in far flung countries, and I saw the empowerment they had gained by giving up their cushy American dreams. I wanted to choose a life as wild as theirs.

Leaving it all for Jesus is a severe and quite polarizing choice. Jesus says in the Bible to count the cost before following Him, but how can we ever really know what such a choice entails?

I didn't really count the cost. I just felt like I should go for it, so I chose to go for it, and now I'm wacky-crazy-pumped yet full of peace. I am choosing to surrender my life, my career, and my future to God. I'll go where God wants me, starting with 11 unknown countries.

11 months before the World Race

I've come up with the following reasons for doing the World Race:

1. To see how God moves in different countries
2. To travel
3. To fall in love with the world and with Jesus—and maybe a boy, if it's God's will
4. To eat new things
5. To live in community
6. To find my calling
7. To see miracles
8. To prove I'm a real Christian, dammit
9. To write a travel blog that changes people's lives and tells the story of how this year changes me
10. To learn
11. To prove I can do it
12. To be interesting and impress people

But also, maybe there isn't much of a reason at all. Maybe I'm doing it because *why the hell not*. No one else knows what to do after college, so maybe it isn't that crazy to sign up for a mission trip. God told me to do it so I'm going to do it, and I don't need to know the ins and outs of why.

When I frame it like that my stomach lurches, so that must be the real reason.

10 months before the World Race

Last night, when my housemates were asleep, I checked the World Race website, and it was finally there: January 2014 Routes.

I gasped. A real, out-loud gasp. I shrunk back from the screen, my hand over my mouth, my stomach clenched.

I climbed out of bed and put my laptop on the floor and hunched over it, like someone was peering over my shoulder.

I clicked.

I read the first route's countries.

It was all countries in Central America.

I was disappointed because I didn't want to go to *Central America*. I wanted to go to faraway places. *Crazy* places. Other hemispheres. Central America sounded…lame.

I read the next two routes, which seemed interesting enough.

But then I read the fourth route's countries and *knew*.

South Africa, Mozambique, Swaziland, India, Nepal, Malaysia, Vietnam, Cambodia, Ireland, Ukraine, and Romania.

What a *wild* way to spend a year.

Nine months before the World Race

Today has been a big doubting day.

My resolution for 2013 was to not question God so much and do better at trusting. But today I just can't. Here's the thing. Religion is weird, and most of the time, I think my religion is probably not true. Do I actually believe it's true? How am I supposed to think all these specific things happened in the Middle East thousands of years ago, and make those things relevant to me and my life? How do I determine if I even buy it?

I consider myself a Christian and I can't even get on board. Cool. And I get like this a lot. Cool. I don't believe in God sometimes. Cool. I'm about to get a world religions degree and then go be a missionary for 11 months so I can tell people to upgrade to my religion. Cool.

What are you thinking, Chelsea?

Seven months before the World Race

I'm excited to tell people about the Race because they'll approve and think I'm a faithful, badass, radical disciple of Jesus who breathes the Holy Spirit and loves with the very heart of God. They'll think I'm choosing to leave my comfortable life to learn who God is by seeing and serving the world, putting aside my preferences for a year, and tossing myself into a life of sacrificial love for all people.

At the same time, I'm scared to tell people because they'll disapprove and think I'm a slacker who hasn't worked any real jobs and is too lazy to try now, not to mention a colonizing, privileged American with a white savior complex who's not using the fancy degree her parents bought her for anything other than the subtle oppression of people groups of whom she has only academic familiarity, if that.

Trying to disregard both feelings. Trying to trust God wants me here. Trying *so* hard not to care what people think.

I have to write a letter to get people to give me $15,500. I have to print hundreds of copies and mail them to everyone I know. Oh, goody.

Five months before the World Race

This is an entry I posted on my World Race blog. I've never blogged before, but I think I'll like it. It's like journaling, but other people read it and compliment you!

Frequently Asked Questions

1. *What's the World Race?*
The World Race is a mission trip to 11 countries in 11 months, and I leave in January of 2014! I have about four months left in the States before heading to South Africa, Mozambique, Swaziland, India, Nepal, Malaysia, Vietnam, Cambodia, Ireland, Ukraine, and Romania.

I'm traveling this route with B Squad. A World Race *squad* is the big group of people who have all signed up for the same route. They are lettered rather than numbered: B Squad is technically "Third-

Generation B Squad" because they've gone through the alphabet two whole times since the first World Race squad ever.

Each squad subdivides into smaller groups, called *teams*, of approximately seven people. Teams stay together for a few months or so and are each sent to a different ministry site in each country. So, while I'll get to know my entire squad well, my teammates will the people I live most closely with.

Each squad has additional leaders who have already done the Race. Some travel with us, and some are back in Georgia overseeing our logistics and general well-being.

2. *What will you do on the Race?*
That will vary. Often, I won't even know until we arrive in each country. My team will be involved with many existing local ministries and people, so each day could look different: construction work, putting on a sports camp, tutoring, preaching, praying, grocery shopping...

3. *Where will you sleep?*
I don't know. We are bringing tents and sleeping bags so we can be prepared to rest anywhere.

4. *What country are you most excited for?*
All of them. Going to so many countries in a year is one of the best things about the Race. But Ireland, India, and Nepal are especially thrilling for me.

5. *How many shots (vaccinations) do you need?*
Lots of shots. Lots and lots. I'm terrified.

6. *How much does it cost?*
$15,500. I'm fundraising to reach this amount, which covers all my expenses once I'm in the field. This is what I'm spending most of my time on now. I've written a letter and mailed it out. I'm writing

this blog. I'm taking people out for coffee. I'm selling t-shirts and bracelets. I'm writing a lot of thank you notes. My first fundraising deadline is in two weeks. By then, I'll need $3500. I'm a little over halfway to that first deadline as I write this.

Fundraising was one of the things I was *not* excited to do. It's hard to ask people for money. But the process has surprised me because I'm starting to see that it's not just about the money. It's about inviting people to be part of something big. It's an exercise in trusting God's provision. It's showing me that I'm not just taking a long vacation all by myself; this is a huge life choice that a lot of people care about.

7. What's the next step?
Training camp. From October 12-19, all January 2014 Racers (not just my squad, but three others, each of which is going to a different set of 11 countries) are going to a camp on the border between Georgia and Tennessee. At training camp, I'll get to meet all my fellow World Racers for the first time. We'll get our first taste of life on the Race, try out our gear, and experience God's heart for the world through prayer, worship, and teaching.

Four months before the World Race
Last night, Dad and I went to REI again. We're always going to REI. After spending a while on the floor testing sleeping pads, I took the Thermarest ProLite Plus home. I cleared a space on my floor and set it down and watched it. It's supposed to be self-inflating, but it's not doing anything.

These are the things about the Race that scare me:
- Getting shots
- Meeting the fundraising deadlines
- Long, claustrophobic bus and plane rides
- Not being able to lie down to sleep on those long, claustrophobic buses and planes. I've been googling how to sleep sitting

up, but the Wikihow is pretty much what you'd expect: "sit up and close your eyes."

- Living near the equator when I'm from the Pacific Northwest and do best with gentle drizzle and 70-degree summers
- Getting sick
- Eating gross stuff
- Losing my Nook and all the books on it
- Ticks
- Getting bored with my clothes
- Liking my team but having to switch to new ones
- Something bad happening to my family back home
- Missing birthdays, weddings, and my sister's high school graduation
- The shock of returning to America at Christmas
- Not making the most of the time given to me
- Saying goodbye to my family and friends in January, uprooting every month, and saying goodbye to my squad at the end of the year
- Forgetting Jesus and turning the World Race into a self-help thing

Four months before the World Race

People have now donated $3500. My sister Kate said it's great that I've met my first fundraising deadline.

"And even if you can't get all the money, Mom and Dad will just pay for it," she said. Then she asked how much Dad makes and I said I didn't know.

It cut me to hear that. *Mom and Dad can just pay for it.* It makes me feel convicted, like I don't need other people or God to go on a mission trip. I don't even need to go on a mission trip. This is just a rich girl's self-help adventure. It's just Christian *Eat, Pray, Love.*

Mom and Dad have made it clear to me that I will go on this trip no matter what. If I don't meet my deadlines, they *will* pay the rest. So I can "trust God to provide," but basically, it's in a lab. The stakes aren't high. It's not real. I have a safety net.

I'm throwing myself into this thing, and I want to actually do that. I've been feeling like I don't want any help from Mom and Dad as far as actual support-raising. Is that trusting, to let God provide, or is it prideful and dumb that I'm rejecting their help? I'm leaning towards not letting them give me anything. They've been buying my equipment and doctor appointments anyway.

Foolish? Maybe. But I want to refuse that safety net. I want to see God provide. It's kind of scary, because at $3500 it feels like the people who would give have already given. How can I raise five times that now?

It just seems to me that $15,500 is not supposed to come from my parents.

Thirty seconds after writing that, I logged onto my fundraising page. It was at $3500 this morning.

Now it's $4123.

Two and a half months before the World Race

When I decided to do the Race it was this big thing, but now that it's turning real, it's just a lot of little specifics. People back home think I'm going to training camp, but what I'm doing is boarding a plane, trying to sleep, drinking a cup of water, hauling my bag, looking for our meeting spot in the atrium at the Atlanta airport, and eating a pizza. Last night I washed my clothes in the sink in my hotel room and hung them to dry over the shower rod, but they're still damp.

I'm about to check out and go to the airport, where I'll meet all the other Racers in the atrium. It's not going to be just B Squad there. There will be four: Y, Z, A, and B. And C, I think, so five. They just made up C Squad after too many people signed up for the other routes. I saw a couple emails about them needing people to switch to it, but they're not going anywhere interesting so I'm sticking with B Squad.

They put us on school buses at the airport and drove us to Tennessee, and everyone was all smiley with nice eyeliner and cute shoes. Basically everyone's a girl on this trip. The bus ride was a couple hours long and I smiled a lot. I sat next to loud people. Enthusiastic. I pretended I liked being loud with strangers.

Dinner was bad. They didn't feed us much.

Two and a half months before the World Race

I was too shocked to sleep last night. I lay in my dark tent amid the silhouettes of my gear, chanting, "What have I done? What have I done?"

I just left B Squad and now I'm on C Squad. I've known from the start that some Racers switch routes before the Race begins, and I've known from the start that I wouldn't be one of them. I loved B Squad's countries: South Africa, Swaziland, Mozambique, India, Nepal, Malaysia, Vietnam, Cambodia, Ireland, Ukraine, and Romania.

But last night, on the first night of training camp, B Squad was asked to gather in the camp's dining hall.

Bill, the World Race boss said, "I think you all know why I'm here. B Squad is the biggest squad and C Squad needs more people. I need three women and three men to move to C Squad tonight. You have three minutes to volunteer, and if at the end of that time no one comes forward, we're drawing names from a hat."

I didn't need three minutes. Just like that, I knew I would move. It wasn't that I wanted to all of a sudden; I just knew it was what I'd do. I stared at the table. I pulled my Bible out and turned pages so it looked like I was praying, but I didn't need to pray.

Things occurred to me—things that could only be described as limp protests that were almost formalities—but my resolve was sudden and firm. My supporters would be confused, my blogs would be incorrect, I wouldn't be able to go to India or Ireland. And wasn't

I already giving up enough for God? Was it really too much to ask that I at least could choose where I went?

Actually, it was too *little* to ask that I could choose where I went. I think that's why the decision was so clear at that moment. I realized that I'd been trusting too much in one thing—my itinerary—to make my trip great, rather than the God who granted it.

I was still staring at my Bible when Bill said, "We're good on girls."

I looked up: while I'd been not reading my Bible, three girls from B Squad had come to the front of the room.

No men had come up, so they drew names and three of our guys joined the girls up front and we all gathered to pray for them and say goodbye. I didn't need to switch after all. Had I just passed a test?

But I felt off as B Squad prayed. I left and told Bill that maybe, possibly, I wanted to switch too. Bill said it was up to me, I could stay or move, but I had to decide now.

So I hesitated, and then suddenly I was saying, "I think I'll switch," in the tone you'd use when picking an ice cream flavor.

And all of a sudden I was swept into the center of B Squad with the other defectors. People I'd known for less than 12 hours cried for us and blessed us. We were taken to a different room where C Squad had been sitting, waiting for their new members to join them. They were clapping and standing when we entered. People with names like Carly and Jacob and Christina shook our hands and hugged and thanked us and as a group, we walked out into the night.

As we headed to our tents that night, I asked someone, "So, where exactly are we going?"

"To bed," someone said.

"No," said another new C Squad member. "Next *year*, where are we going?"

We didn't know. We'd just switched routes and we didn't even know where we'd signed up to go.

Well, it turns out we are going to Honduras, Guatemala, El Salvador, Bulgaria, Albania, Zambia, Malawi, Mozambique, Thailand, Cambodia, and Malaysia. Mozambique, Cambodia, and Malaysia are the only countries that remain of my original itinerary. I never had any particular interest in Central America—it sounds boring and too close to America—and now I'm going to spend three months there. I had to find Bulgaria, Albania, and Zambia on a map.

One day ago, I thought I was going to South Africa in January. Now, I'm going to Honduras.

It's *so* loud at this camp. Lots of people talking. They just met. How are they this friendly? Gosh, I'm so hungry.

The World Race staff introduced an exercise today to prepare us for travel mishaps. They had our squad put all our stuff on two tarps. Then they covered one tarp up and were like, "Oh no! The airline lost half your baggage! You have to get through 24 hours without your stuff now."

My bag was one of the "lost" ones, so I introduced myself to Heidi from New Mexico. She was pulling a tent and sleeping bag from her pack. She invited me into her tent for the night and we tried to fit the two of us into her mummy sleeping bag and I couldn't believe how generous she was. She gave me warm socks and pants.

Some of the guys, Dillon and a couple others, are planning to sleep on pieces of cardboard by the campfire.

Two and a half months before the World Race
I'm not happy with you, God.

They're all about listening to the Holy Spirit here. That's not new to me, but it's only one facet of my spirituality and for some of these people, it seems like that's the only way they express their faith. That's hard for me because I think I'm not wired to be super spiritual all the time.

But they said it was bigger than that, and of course I want to feel the ecstasy they say is possible with God's presence, so I put my hands out and begged to be filled with the Holy Spirit like they instructed us. How could I have made it any clearer? But nothing happened. I was just sitting there with my hands out, getting frustrated. I went through all sorts of mental gymnastics to feel chills or cry or something, but I felt nothing.

I tried saying sorry for wanting to know data more than wanting to know God, because maybe I'm too book smart for the Holy Spirit to take over me... but that didn't work. I don't know what I'm supposed to say to get God to make me feel how I want to feel. It seemed like God's presence was overwhelming everyone but me.

I said, "I surrender all." It didn't work, so I'm giving up for today.

Two and a half months before the World Race
I'm not making the most of training camp. I'm not being impressive or stepping up as a leader. I'm not cheering and yelling all the time, or letting my radiant personality shine. I signed up for the World Race but this feels like summer camp in cold rain with sadistic counselors and no food. I'm a loser here. I'll have no friends this year.

"For heaven's sake," they told us today during a session about blogging and fundraising, "don't publish writing about your poop. It scares your mommies and daddies and it's bad marketing. People won't want to donate money if you only want to talk about your diarrhea and parasites.

"And don't think you're the solution to the world's problems," they also said. "Don't get white savior complexes. You're there to witness what God is *already* doing."

"And don't be a dirty idiot," they said. "Take showers. Be street smart. Be presentable. You know. Don't be a dirty idiot."

We've spent hours every day worshipping this week. The worship team delights me. They produce this sloppy, joyful din that tires me out and energizes me and makes me want to lift weights and write books and kiss people. They sing original, simple, strong, and true songs. Everyone takes turns singing; there's no bearded white guy with a guitar in charge of everything. There are guitars, a violin, viola, flute, djembe, box drum, tambourine, wall—as in, one guy slaps it—and reindeer bells. One person is onstage dancing—not a choreographed liturgical routine with streamers—she just jumps all over the place like she's in a mosh pit. One of the leaders wears handmade anklets with bells on them. He stomps his feet hard and bells pop off and roll around.

It made me realize that I should bring an instrument with me on the field. I have the mandolin Grammy and Papa gave me. I can't play it but I think I'll bring it anyway.

Two and a half months before the World Race
C Squad was split into seven teams today. Mine named itself Crisco. Like grease, like oil, like anointing, like Jesus Christ, the Anointed One.

There's this girl on my team, Kori. She said she's had oil come from her hands before.

"Really?" I asked. I wasn't sure if she was being figurative or not.

"Yes. Literally," she said.

"Supernaturally?"

"Yes."

I thought that might have been an opportunity to trust God, stop questioning so much, keep an open mind...

My team also has Tony, David, Michelle, and Robyn. I like them. Tony's the leader. He says he managed four KFCs in Minnesota and likes to brag about how he'd always scrape the black mold off just in time for health inspections.

This afternoon, we were put in our teams and told to go "make a memory." The six of us drove to the river they rafted in the 1996

27

Atlanta Olympics and looked at the water. We went to Piggly Wiggly. We went to a restaurant attached to a gas station and ate a lot of pizza, which tasted great but gave us stomach aches after eating so little all week.

Soon, training camp will be over. I'll go back home and have the holidays with my family. Then, I'll reunite with these people and go. It's strange.

Seven weeks before the World Race
One of the team leaders is stepping down from the Race so they need someone to be the leader and they called and asked me.

I feel like switching squads is enough. Why one more thing?

Six weeks before the World Race
Already, the Race is not what I expected. Not only am I going to different countries, I'm going to be a team leader.

"What do you think? Should I do the leading thing?" I asked Kristal, my oldest friend.

"You can take it or not; I don't think there's a right answer," she said. "But if you choose the more challenging option, God may have more space to work in you."

That settled it. I emailed the appropriate people and said I would do it.

My teammate David suffered a bad back injury and won't be leaving in January, so without us two, they're disbanding Crisco and spreading the members out across the other teams.

My new team is Brazen Hearts. I think it's kind of a dumb name, but they seem excited about it. I'm going to really miss Crisco and I'm not thrilled about being on an all-girl team.

Three days before the World Race
Mom and Dad and I fly to Atlanta tomorrow.

Today, I woke up. I hung out with Kate on the couch and watched YouTube videos.

I looked at the mess on my floor and thought, *I need to pack.* I decided I needed more underwear.

I questioned whether I *really* wanted to bring the mandolin.

I ate lunch and watched a movie with Mom and Kate, and sewed up the rips in my orange sarong. I can use my sarong as a scarf, blanket, or towel.

I went to Target for bug spray and underwear and swung by Starbucks at sunset. Mt. Rainier was pink and orange and I said goodbye to it.

I let Dad spray permethrin on my clothes. He told me that the permethrin would only last 42 washes and I told him that probably wouldn't be an issue.

The whole family ate dinner together.

I spent *forever* putting things in my pack the right way. I weighed it and felt smug when it clocked in at 38 pounds.

It's 2:00 a.m. and I'm going to sleep.

Two days before the World Race

It's 2:15 a.m. and I can't sleep.

I was trying to pray and I'm opening my eyes now and looking out my bedroom window. I'm going to miss this land of tall, jagged trees. I'm going to miss how everything is green, from the moss on the trees, to the pine needles, to the algae in the pond, to the wet grass.

One day before the World Race

Squads Y, Z, A, B, and C are in an airport hotel. Lots of backpacks and yelling and praying. Lots of unidentifiable emotions.

Saying goodbye to Mom and Dad was hard. The hardest part was how tightly they hugged me and how sad they were.

They have to go home now and miss me. I get to do something epic.

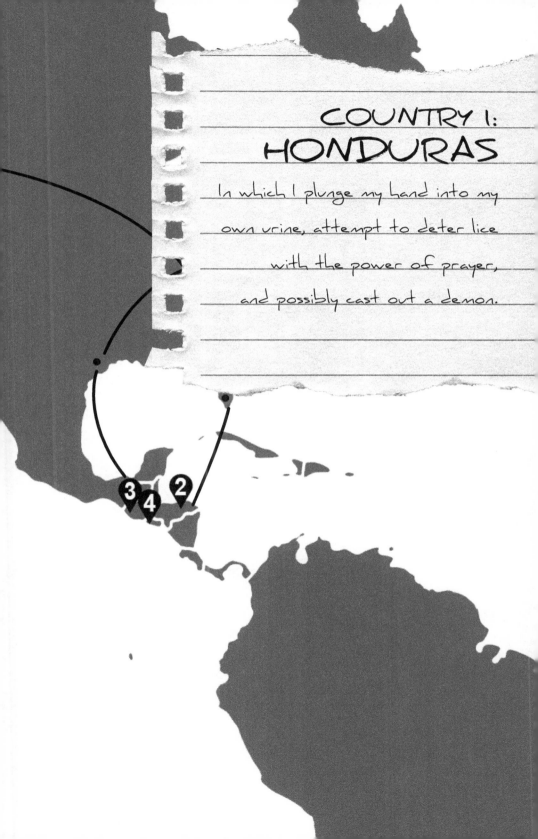

COUNTRY 1:
HONDURAS

In which I plunge my hand into my own urine, attempt to deter lice with the power of prayer, and possibly cast out a demon.

January 9
La Ermita, a village north of Tegucigalpa, Honduras
What just happened.

We woke up in Atlanta. Then we were in Miami. Then we boarded a plane and our pilot announced that the descent would involve a lot of sharp turns and sudden braking.

I don't normally clap when planes land, but today I joined the relieved applause as we skidded to our gate in Tegucigalpa, the capital of Honduras.

Four of the six C Squad teams were told to look for a woman named Gracie, who would be hosting us at her ministry site in a village 90 minutes away. The two teams who were with different ministries hastily bade the rest of us goodbye and disappeared with strangers.

We found Gracie at baggage claim. She had purple streaks in her blonde hair, and she was tan and muscled. We exchanged no pleasantries until she'd ushered us through the airport and out to a bus and a pickup truck in the parking lot. The truck bed was full of Little Caesars pizzas and bottles of warm Coke, and we devoured them as if we hadn't seen American food in years, even though it had been only hours.

Then, Gracie put us on the bus and our bags in the truck bed, and we drove through bad traffic and stinky air until the roads opened up and we were on hilly roads on the outskirts of the city. Tegucigalpa's pastel houses sprawled forever in all directions. The sky was cloudy but the sun shot through it.

We drove until we came to a place called La Ermita. We drove its lone, lumpy road and stopped at a small cinder block compound behind a tall black gate. This was our first ministry site.

The sun was gone by now. It was cloudy and raining hard. *So, this is how it starts*, I thought.

We entered the compound with our bags and were instructed to put our belongings in the rooms on the second story. It was scary to get up there in the rain. I was wearing my 65-liter pack on my back, my 25-liter daypack on my front, and my mandolin over my shoulder. I climbed a slippery, rickety staircase—so steep, it was nearly a ladder—and alighted on an outdoor concrete balcony. There was no railing to keep us from falling, but there was a power strip.

My team, Brazen Hearts, went into a doorless, windowless, unlit cinder block room filled with bunk beds. I unpacked my tent and twisty-tied it into a bottom bunk to keep mosquitoes out. I put my journal and my daypack inside and climbed into its meshy embrace and zipped it up and that's where I am now.

I don't want to come out. I don't want to help anyone with anything. I don't want to do mission work. I don't want to be a leader. I want to sleep and read and be left alone. I'm tired and freaked out and disoriented.

It's getting dark quickly. It didn't occur to me that we wouldn't get twilight at this latitude.

They'll feed us dinner soon, and then we'll meet in another cinder block room so Gracie can brief us on what the hell we've signed ourselves up for.

I can process one thing at a time. Despite my feelings, I'm also thankful because my need for the Lord is desperate and real.

The air is thick with bugs.

It looks like there are going to be two places I can be alone this month: on the toilet and in the shower. I haven't taken a shower yet, but my very first pee in Central America, I forgot that we weren't supposed to flush toilet paper and threw it in the bowl.

"Shit," I hissed to myself. I wasn't sure if the toilet would back up, so I decided to get it out.

A single Barbie leg, of all things, happened to be on the back of the toilet. I used that to try fishing it out, but the paper began dissolving. So I put the leg down and shook my hand really fast and gave myself a pep talk.

"I am not a slave to fear!" I declared under my breath. "I am a beloved daughter of the Most High! I am a badass!" When I was sufficiently pumped up, I thrust my entire forearm into my urine and scooped out the now-pulpy paper. Pee splashed all over the toilet seat, and now I have to remember not to chew my cuticles until I find purified water.

January 10
La Ermita, Honduras

I woke up feeling rested at 7:00. We had cornflakes and crappy coffee for breakfast.

Gracie and her husband Lee operate this ministry primarily as a children's home and refuge for young women pregnant from rape and incest. This month, we are going to do construction projects on the property, spend time with the women and kids who live here, and go into the village to find families in need of food and medicine. Some food program is offering help to those in need, but they need volunteers to go out and find people.

But the first mission work I'll be doing on the Race is bathing a puppy named Sasha. Sasha has sharp claws and is almost cute. Right now, she's jumping all over those of us who have chosen to workout in the courtyard. They've put on an *Insanity* workout video to stave off missionary bodies.

Missionary bodies are the things everyone is afraid of. Missionary bodies aren't tan and sinewy like you might think. They're flabby and undernourished, the kind of bodies that can't afford gym memberships or protein. They're pale and sweaty from wearing modest clothes in hot places.

We walked through town but it's just that single road. Everyone said, "*Hola!*" and I was catcalled more in 15 minutes than I had been my entire life. A lot of men yelled, "*Puta!*" and I think that's bad. I wish I knew Spanish. I feel helpless.

So far, my favorite part of the World Race is standing on the second level of the compound and washing my face. I did it today and looked around while I was up there. Our travel hammocks were hanging between concrete posts, and people were dangling their legs off the second story and sitting on the roof. I could see the shy, petite Honduran women and Gracie milling about below. I captured the snapshot in my mind: the gate behind them, the big colorful plants, the houses, the mountains on the horizon, and the sky.

January 11
La Ermita, Honduras
Gracie gathered us outside tonight for a worship service, even though it was about to rain, because God told her to.

"So *I* said, 'God, you have to tell those storm clouds to move out,'" said Gracie. "See, you have to press in like that. When God tells you to do something, do it and trust that He will make it possible. When He promises something, call Him on it, and press into it against the obstacles."

My instinct would be to say, "*Well*, Gracie, it seems you may have just been thinking wishfully about the service and maybe God didn't promise you anything… and anyway, it's not a big deal whether we worship inside or outside."

But the clouds *did* move out, so what do I know.

Gracie also told us that we were starting a long journey, and we would have to take it one day at a time. She said that when we grew tired and worried, we needed to worship God.

I want to be like Gracie. I want to increase my faith by claiming big things from God.

January 12
La Ermita, Honduras
We are going to the mall today! I think there will be WiFi there!

There *was* WiFi, plus a Dunkin' Donuts.

We're on the bus back to La Ermita now, and the people who aren't jamming to Old Crow Medicine Show are telling their testimonies.

If a testimony is the story of your life and how you came to Jesus, then I've never told mine. I feel like I don't even *have* one after hearing some of the things God has brought my squadmates through. Compared to them, I've had it easy: not too much death, no abuse or sex or drugs or discrimination or poverty. I can't even remember the moment I became a Christian. This makes me feel inferior, because I don't have as powerful a story to tell. It makes me feel ashamed, as if I haven't earned the right to be serving here.

I want to know my story, or the story of what Jesus has done in me. I'm sure I have one. I'm praying that it glorifies God and not me.

January 13
La Ermita, Honduras
I finally posted a blog about settling in here, and it took over an hour to upload with our internet stick.

Hot showers don't come easily, either. There is no running water. Big barrels collect rainwater, and when we want to bathe, we dip old paint buckets in and haul them to the stalls. If we want the water to be warm, we fill the buckets in the morning and leave them on the steps all day in the sun.

The internet stick is annoying and it's unnerving to be isolated from email and social media, but the water thing doesn't bother me much at all.

January 14
La Ermita, Honduras
The devil tried to make me stop reading the Bible today by making me want to poop.

Normally, I wouldn't blame something like that on the devil, but people here seem to put a lot of stock in spiritual things. So when I was praying and reading my Bible this morning, feeling God's presence, and then my stomach started hurting, I wondered if maybe it *was* Satan.

So I stayed with the Bible, refusing to be distracted from God, and I stayed there, reading and praying. The feeling went away when the devil saw I wasn't gonna go to the toilet. Then I had a nice time with Jesus.

January 17
La Ermita, Honduras
There are young sisters who live here named Ivonia and Erica. They have cerebral palsy. They spend their entire days on black gym mats. They have lice. They don't talk and they can't walk. My teammate Kelly is a speech therapist, so she's giving them exercises to help them communicate. She's angry about their living conditions.

I watched Ivonia and Erica today, and by the time I was done, I was depressed and sleepy and grossed out. But I played my mandolin a little with them, the three chords I know, and Lacey said that it made Jesus smile.

I wish I could have Mom and Dad give them thousands of dollars for wheelchairs and therapists. Or I wish I could forget how depressing it was to be with them.

But I couldn't fix them or ignore them. I had to sit with them.

January 18
La Ermita, Honduras
Before dinner I went to do laundry at the *pila*, which is the concrete basin we wash clothes in. On the way there, I stopped by Ivonia and Erica's room. One of their new nannies was with them and I poked my head in and said hello.

The nanny, Novia, was frustrated. Erica was sick and irritable. Novia was trying to feed her and she said it was *muy difícil*.

Even though it was so hard to be there yesterday, I wanted to stay. I sat for awhile not doing anything helpful. The power went out. Novia and I talked a little. People came in and out. Finally I asked Novia, "*Puedo orar contigo* (Can I pray with you)?" and I did my best to use Spanish words but mostly I prayed in English. I didn't pray for anything big or bold or specific.

I'm in bed about to fall asleep, but I was just brushing my teeth and needed to fart. I let one *rip*, and then I realized I was in front of the doorway to the guys' room. I don't know if any of them were awake.

January 21
La Ermita, Honduras

I've noticed something. A lot of my squadmates are scared of getting lice, so they *rebuke* the lice. They rebuke them in Jesus' name.

In fact, they rebuke a lot of things in Jesus' name. And claim a lot of things. Kind of like what Gracie did with the clouds.

I don't get it. I didn't know we could demand comforts based on our specific neuroses. I'm always asking for things when I pray, but I've never prayed the way some of these people do.

When we arrived, Gracie declared that in Jesus' name, none of us would get sick, and part of me felt relieved and safe.

But then I wondered what we were supposed to do if what we claim in Jesus' name doesn't come true? Does that indicate weak faith? Weak God?

Lots of my squadmates hear directly from God when they pray and I feel lame because I don't as often. Plus, I don't speak in tongues or get visions.

But maybe it's because a lot of them are from the American South, and they are from different church cultures. I'm a Pacific Northwest Lutheran. So, is it a personal failing that I feel weird about praying like that, or just a difference in culture?

January 22
La Ermita, Honduras

Brazen Hearts has spent this week out in the villages knocking on strangers' doors. A food organization is teaming up with our ministry host to give young mothers food and medications, so our team goes into villages with clipboards and questionnaires. We go house to house and ask in broken Spanish if a pregnant woman or baby lives there. If the household meets either qualification, we record the mother's information and the food organization makes arrangements to meet their nutritional and medical needs.

After the survey is completed, my team offers to sing a song. Oddly, no one seems to find this weird. I bring out my mandolin and we sing "Open the Eyes of My Heart" in Spanish or "Amazing Grace" in English.

Finally, we offer to pray for the family. Usually Nicole spearheads this, but if she isn't there, it's up to the rest of us.

"What things for to pray I you health or family?" we ask in broken Spanish.

We pray in English for the parents and kids and anoint them with oil, making a cross on their foreheads. "*Bendiciones,*" we tell them. "Blessings." Often, they make crosses on our foreheads and bless us back.

Today all six of us were walking through Talanga, the town closest to La Ermita. We found ourselves at the house of a woman named Marta.

Marta is a grandmother who lives with her daughter and granddaughter. Their family didn't fit our requirements for the food program, but we stayed and chatted anyway. She sat us on their sofas in the sitting room and turned off the TV. Marta showed us a basket someone had given her for her birthday, which was full of nice notes and pictures, and she showed us a picture of her family. She gave us coffee and cookies. She let us hold her granddaughter. We prayed together. We stayed for one hour.

I was skeptical about door-to-door ministry before coming here. I considered it presumptuous and rude to share Jesus with strangers whose language I couldn't speak. Plus, in America, knocking on doors is weird. And frankly, pretty annoying.

But as I've begun this work, I have to admit that while my doubts remain, I've seen a strange grace in the disarming hospitality of everyone we meet. The power dynamics I feared aren't materializing. The awkwardness is friendly, not forceful. We haven't been telling people what to believe. We've been looking at photo albums, playing soccer, and learning songs. My team goes to strangers' doors with curiosity and humility, and because of the grace in the strangers' hearts, they invite us inside and assure us that we, the strangers, are guests and not invaders.

January 23
La Ermita, Honduras
Today we cast out a demon.

Kelly missed the whole event because she was caring for Ivonia and Erica, so when the rest of us came back from town, our team sat at a picnic table to tell her about it.

"We went to a house with the survey," I said, "and there was a lady there who lived with her 22-year-old daughter named Teresa, who wasn't in at the moment, and a month-old granddaughter. She was talking about how the baby's dad had disappeared, and Teresa was suffering from postpartum depression."

"To get clinical help, she has to go all the way to Tegucigalpa, which is expensive," said Nicole. "We were asking the normal food survey questions. I was holding the baby. And then Teresa came in. She'd been out for groceries. She was obviously not expecting us to be there, holding her baby. We said hello, and we finished the survey. Then the grandmother, Juana, prayed for us. We gathered around them and put our hands on their shoulders and prayed for them. We were just praying nice things, and Teresa was shaking a little bit. Nothing weird at first, but then, pretty quickly, she started shaking... like, a lot. Her hand was jerking. She was sweating and getting really hot. It was clearly *not* from God. We prayed for a long time.

"We recited Scripture," Nicole continued. "We broke out in song. I started praying in Spanish. We were praying, battling whatever was showing up. It wasn't from God."

"When we said 'Jesus,' she shook more," said Lacey.

"It was at least a half hour," said Kelsey.

"Or 45 minutes," said Lacey.

"I thought it was important for me to pray in Spanish, so she could understand," said Nicole. "I kept telling her the Lord loved her, that He wanted her to be free of whatever the devil was doing to her. Kori kept getting words and visions from God about how much freedom He had for her. But the harder we prayed, the more she shook."

"And she was so hot," said Kelsey. "She was dripping sweat."

"A couple times we asked her, 'How are you doing?'" Lacey said. "She replied, 'I'm very good.'"

"'What are you hearing?' we'd say."

"And she'd say, 'That Jesus loves me.'

"And we said, 'Are you hearing anything else that's not from Jesus?' She said she wasn't, then she seemed to get confused—"

"She was trying to say something," said Kori, "but whatever was inside her wasn't allowing her to tell the truth, and I really sensed that when she said 'I'm fine,' I knew she *wasn't* fine."

"Then she said, 'I don't know what's happening. I can't control this.' There was a spirit of confusion in the room, and I felt sick to my stomach, but I knew we were supposed to press through and keep praying, and all of us said to each other, 'We're not leaving.' We were still praying, saying the name of Jesus, but nothing was happening. We didn't know what to do."

"Then I was overwhelmed with the need to read the Bible, and I read, 'Whatsoever you bind on earth will be bound in heaven, and whatsoever you loose on earth will be loosed in heaven,'[1] and I felt something fierce rise up inside me. I thought, *That's it; we're gonna bind*

---

1. Matthew 18:18

this thing right now. And so I put a hand on her and said, 'We're all agreeing that this thing be bound up,' and almost immediately she—"

"It was her face…" we murmured.

"Had the most peaceful look…"

"Her head rested on my shoulder…"

"She stopped shaking…"

"She collapsed on Nicole and looked like she was in this peaceful sleep," said Lacey.

"I held her in my arms like a baby," said Nicole. "For maybe a half hour."

"The peace of God fell," said Kori. "The atmosphere shifted in seconds, and all the confusion, the chaos, anxiety, it was all gone, and it was like Jesus himself was standing there."

"Then the grandmother, Juana, started giving all of us hugs," I said. "She grabbed my hands and we both just started bawling. She had thick black eyeliner and it was running down her cheeks. And I didn't understand what she was saying but she kept touching my face and my head and kept hugging me and kissing me and I—"

"She was saying the most beautiful things to you, Chels," said Nicole. "She said she felt like your hands were the hands of God, and the hands were touching her, and she couldn't control her crying. And Chelsea was bawling—"

"*I* was trying not to cry," said Lacey.

"I was crying," said Nicole.

"And when we were getting ready to leave, Teresa, the one that was delivered, told us, 'I want to sing over *you*.' And she sang a song we didn't know. And then we left."

"And that's all we did," I said. We were exhausted. We went to the park. We were hungry. But what I felt more than anything was this *stability*. I felt grounded and solid and heavy in a good way."

I feel like God is sitting across from me, smirking, waiting for a response. It's like God is asking, "Well, what did you think of *that*? What are you going to put in your diary now?"

Well… I've never seen that before. Always believed it could happen. Never thought I'd see it. *It* being… what, an exorcism? Deliverance? Breakthrough? I don't know what to call it.

I *do* know two things. I know that when we were in the thick of it, I didn't feel very strong or spiritual or anything at all, but I *was* determined to stay right there. No one could have persuaded me to leave. And I know that when Juana held my hands and cried and looked at me with her eyeliner all over the place, I had this sense that I was looking at God.

Sometimes I wonder if I hold the group back and keep God from working as powerfully as possible because I don't *believe* enough. I feel like I didn't contribute anything to this thing that happened. I just happened to be there, and I knew I had to stay, but I didn't feel inspired or supernatural.

I feel like God is telling me to stop fixating on my faith. Telling me, the skeptic who needs to look at everything, to look to Him, to stop paying attention to myself, to stop trying to "level up" my spirituality to match the way it manifests in other people.

January 27
La Ermita, Honduras

Every day, we go in clumps across the street to the pulpería, a little shop run from someone's house. We go there to get cookies, plantain chips, and chocolate milk. We ask for "*Coca en bolsa*," and they pour Cokes into plastic bags so they can keep the glass bottles.

There are houses painted like Sprite and Fanta cans. People get money for turning their houses into advertisements. Dillon says that buying a house like that down here would only cost a thousand bucks.

The public buses here are old American school buses that have been pimped out with lights and glitter and speakers and Bible verses. They call them chicken buses, and I don't know if that's because there are always people transporting their chickens on them, or because… I don't know why they're called chicken buses.

There are stray dogs everywhere and they're not cute. They're pests. They come around when we sit on the side of the road eating chicken, so we yell at them until they go away.

As I've been writing this, a chicken bus drove by. Even with the flashing lights and chrome, it still retained the words "Tulsa School District" on its side.

I feel so far from home, but we're still on the same landmass. If I took enough time, I could drive to Oklahoma.

January 28
La Ermita, Honduras

Everyone on Brazen Hearts slept badly last night. Even *I* slept badly. The last few days, some of us haven't been able to sleep here or there, but it's getting worse. Kori dreamt of bad angels coming toward us. I was up for hours scratching at bug bites.

The consensus seems to be that it's a spiritual attack brought on by our boldness in ministry and Teresa's deliverance.

We gathered in our bedroom, and we prayed over our beds, that the demons attacking us would leave and that we'd sleep. We anointed our pillows with oil.

Normally, I wouldn't blame Satan for a bad night's sleep, but... the world's different down here, so I'm just going to try these words on:

Okay, Jesus. In Your name I pray, let me get no new mosquito bites tonight. In Your name, may no mosquitoes come near me—I feel weird praying this, but I feel like You want me to, and I really don't want any more bites. So, uh... we claim Your rest, Jesus. We claim a perfect night's sleep and absolute protection from bugs. Amen.

Ugh.

The Bible says our fight isn't against the visible but the invisible, but the visible sure is what we get hung up on. We pray over all the visible stuff, and when our prayers don't come true, when we get the mosquito bites anyway, we say, "Such earthly matters hold no power over us! We are born of the Spirit, not of the flesh, so we don't even care anyway!"

Maybe it's not that God isn't powerful when we still get bug bites. Maybe it's that it doesn't *matter* when we get bug bites. Maybe it's that we shouldn't be treating God like a vending machine. Maybe we forget that our God became a person who got bug bites and had prayer requests denied, too. Maybe we are trying to forget that Jesus suffered because we don't think we should have to.

This whole claiming things in Jesus' name... I don't buy it. But we keep hearing of times when God *did* grant dumb prayers. Like the storm kept at bay for Gracie, or the hundred times I've seen my mom pray for a good parking spot only to have one immediately open up. I believe that God cares for us, down to the littlest detail. God's love is not reserved for great feats. God lives in us and loves us deeper than anything, so maybe God *does* want to give us what we desire...

Maybe I'm just mucking around in semantics now.

I trust that Jesus is somehow bigger than my little faith and our weird rhetoric around prayer. I wouldn't be *here* if I didn't trust Jesus. I mean, I wouldn't be in a Honduran village covered in mosquito bites, playing a mandolin and singing in bad Spanish in town squares, and casting out demons, if I didn't have faith.

Being a Christian is weird. It's compelling, sure, and the longer I'm in it, the wilder life gets. But I can't deny that it's a bizarre thing to hang my reality on.

January 29
La Ermita, Honduras
We're tired. My feet are lumpy with mosquito bites. I'm almost out of snack cash.

It's the last day of ministry. Lacey and I had to burn trash out back in the eucalyptus groves. We used up a whole matchbook trying to get the wet diapers to catch fire but we couldn't.

I don't like the *work* part of mission work.

I sat on the roof and read my Bible. I read all of Paul's letter to the Ephesians. I had just started on the Gospel of Mark when Dillon came and sat down next to me. He had my mandolin. I've barely played it this month because he has been borrowing it.

He was noodling on it for a few minutes, but then he took out his phone and we listened to the Avett Brothers for a while. We talked a little about his past, and how he got saved, and the Race, but mostly we were just sitting on the roof listening to American music.

This month has been murky. I've just spent three weeks in an unfamiliar country. On top of being team leader and keeping our logistics and budget in check, my world suddenly whorls with devils and angels. I'm tired. So for once, it was nice not to discuss the demons in the mattresses or the upcoming travel day, and to just listen to music.

January 31
La Ermita, Honduras

Tomorrow the other two teams get here and we leave for Antigua, Guatemala, for the first of five debriefs. Debriefs are breaks in between ministries to stay in hostels, tour a little, rest, and prepare for the next month of ministry.

I bought a *lot* of homemade plantain chips at the pulpería for the bus ride.

Sasha, the puppy, drank the water we were using to rinse paint brushes and died. She was so annoying. We all feel awful.

COUNTRY 2:
GUATEMALA

In which I work in a hospital,

briefly own a pet,

and eat street food.

③ ④ ②

February 1

On the way to Antigua, Guatemala

Twelve hours ago, around 3:00 a.m., two armed guards escorted C Squad a mile down the single road of La Ermita to a football field where there was a space big enough for a bus to park. We waited awhile, and then a pair of headlights ripped through the night and the bus came into view.

I heard this is considered a luxury bus. I guess the seats are squishy, but the bathroom is out of order and there isn't any air conditioning. The ride will take 15 hours, plus one or two more for bathroom breaks and the border crossings into and out of El Salvador, which lies between Honduras and Guatemala.

I woke up after two hours of napping just as the sky was lightening. My stomach hurt. Hoping it was from hunger and not motion sickness, I dug into my snack stash of plantain chips, stale cheesy popcorn, a large packet of soursop knock-off Kool Aid mix, and 18 cookies. I started on the cookies.

Kori told me the other day that she ate over 150 cookies in January, and I didn't believe her. Then she did the math: we ate cookies every afternoon and almost every morning with our coffee. At pulperías we bought Chokis, which come in packs of six, and Chikys, which come in packs of four. And then during team time, Brazen Hearts always had extra cookies to share, so Kori is right.

I'm sitting next to a guy named Henry. He's not a World Racer, but he plans to become a missionary and is going to stay with some missionaries in Antigua for several months. He's nice, but I only sat next to him because I mistook his backpack for Tony's and I wanted to sit with Tony. Our teams weren't together this month and I missed talking to him.

Henry taught me about Honduras' national seal and the people represented on the money. Then he moved on to wildlife. "There are animals in the mountains, like... I forget how to say it in English." Henry mimed what I thought were ears.

"Rabbits?" I guessed.

"No, they're bigger."

"Cats?"

"No, Santa Claus uses them."

"Reindeer?"

"Yes."

"You have reindeer in Honduras?"

"Yes," said Henry. "People hunt them and put their"—he mimed antlers—"in their homes."

Then Henry took a nap.

It's hot on the bus. I rubbed peppermint oil on my face. It cooled me off, but the invigorating scent woke up Henry and now we are going to have to revisit the reindeer issue.

I saw a perfectly conical volcano. Its summit is shrouded in clouds. Henry said it was a dangerous one. It didn't look like Mt. Rainier at all—it had no snow and the ground around it was flat. It looked like a diagram of a volcano in a textbook.

I know that there are hours and hours left on this bus. When we get to Antigua, tired and hungry and grumpy and behind schedule, our legs will be stiff and we'll be stressed. I'll do all my team leader duties, like changing money and buying cell phone minutes and making rational decisions about our food, and I'll be too tired to focus on it well. But for now, I am enjoying the ride.

February 2

That wasn't 15 hours on a bus. That was 24 hours on a bus.

We drove into Antigua at who knows what time. It was night. The buildings were short and colorful and the roads were bumpy. There was a parade going on when we arrived in town. People were wearing huge animal costumes, but they were only lit from the waist down by car headlights, so only dingy fake lion and horse legs were visible.

Evil spirits are one thing, but traveling *itself* is rough. I stayed up so late with the other team leaders running around converting currency and getting cell phone minutes I was on the verge of sobbing from exhaustion.

It's at the end of travel days I want to quit this.

February 2
Antigua, Guatemala

I could have cried when we saw our coaches, Sharon and Bobby. They live in Texas, but they counsel our entire squad from the States, and come to all our debriefs to visit in person. They are my parents' age, and they are kind and they hug us and they smell good and I bet all their travel shampoos are brand new and not diluted with water.

I wish I could explore this city alone. I already want to come back here someday. I don't want to leave here in a few days to work at a government-run hospital in the mountains. I'm scared that this debrief won't allow time for enjoying this place.

So God, relax me; take care of me. Refresh me, because right now I don't want to do mission work next month. I want to be a normal backpacker and stay in this hostel with the blue hammocks and palm trees, and I want to talk to other backpackers and go out and drink coffee and wine all day.

It should have been an easy day, but I had to play around with the team budget for next month and I felt like I was cheated of the free time I needed so badly.

Antigua's streets are cobblestones and even the stone gutters running down their middles like spines are charming. You can see Volcán de Agua through the Santa Catalina Arch, which is white and yellow, like the church of La Merced, whose facade has such detailed reliefs it could be made of lace. Bakeries and coffee shops abound and everything is cheap and small. The Mayan people are short and stout and wrapped in heavy, colorful, patterned linen.

There are beautiful backpackers here from the States and Europe and Australia. The women wear crop tops revealing strong, happy bellies, and they have beads in their hair and tan legs and easy smiles. The men have sunlit, scruffy beards and shining blue eyes and worn-out baseball caps and big packs packed lightly. I wish I could be with them. I wish I could *be* them. We could sit around and take a break from being so serious and working so hard and I wouldn't have to do ministry.

The night is filled with gold Spanish architecture, and candles burn in sconces on pink and gold stucco. It smells like trash and bread and coffee and smoke. The night air is warm and the breeze is cool but not cold.

And *tonight*, I was proud to be an American. I always *like* being an American, but I'm never really proud. But tonight, after dinner at Pollo Campero, at a rooftop bar, the Seattle Seahawks beat the Denver Broncos in the Super Bowl, and I don't care about football, but when *that* happened, I screamed and chanted and jumped and hugged everyone. Someone bought a round of disgusting red-orange shots and we choked them down, cheering all the while. Lacey is the only other squad-mate from Washington, so we especially celebrated.

I'll be sad to leave Antigua.

February 6
Santa Cruz del Quiché, Guatemala

Apparently we almost died on the way to our second ministry location.

C Squad had a chicken bus all to ourselves, and we were driving to Santa Cruz del Quiché, up in the mountains. The road was narrow and rocky, and the bus was rickety. Through the dirty windows, we gazed into deep valleys.

Apparently, at one point, the brakes gave out on the chicken bus and it almost drove off a cliff. Everyone freaked out. I don't mean that everyone was *nervous*. I mean that a lot of them were *certain* we were about to die.

But I didn't notice. Lacey and Tony and I were talking in the back of the bus. I smelled the scorching brakes, sure, and we slid back down the road on those precipitous hairpin turns now and then, but I figured that was normal.

But once we came to flatter ground, people were jumping out of the bus to cry and catch their breaths.

And of course, it wasn't just a sketchy bus ride; it was a *demonic attack*.

Why didn't I notice? Should I have? I felt no attack. Yet they all said that's what it was. Is this another example of my deplorable spiritual insensitivity? I don't really want to get "better" at feeling attacked by demons. I want to get better at being a source of peace and joy. Besides, I have a hard enough time believing in God. I don't have the bandwidth to give this much credit to Satan, too.

February 7
Santa Cruz del Quiché, Guatemala
Julie is our ministry host here in Quiché. She's not as in-your-face as Gracie from La Ermita, but she also comes off as a badass who doesn't take shit from Satan. She's short and round and has a can-I-speak-with-the-manager haircut.

She said that the ministry here has been under a lot of spiritual attack lately, so naturally, we should watch out.

We're living on a compound again, but this one is bigger, and anyone can enter it, because it's right next to the hospital. So people walk all around, selling trinkets and buying sodas from food stands. They're not *pulperías* here, but *tiendas*.

The modest, single-story government hospital sprawls to the left after the gate. There's a big field on the right where we've pitched our 41 tents, and straight ahead, a low-roofed concrete building with hot showers and an outdoor kitchen. There is a white awning set up, and underneath it, we play Dutch Blitz and Monopoly Deal.

We can exit the compound, past the guard who doesn't pay attention to anything and the woman selling cups of fresh fruit, which we are not supposed to eat. There's an internet cafe across the street, and if we turn right and keep walking, there is a little food cart called *Hamburguesa Mundo*. We're not supposed to eat there either. Toward the center of town is yet another food cart offering *mixtas*. *Mixtas* are skewers of shriveled-up ambiguous meat bits that sizzle on a skillet all day. *Mixtas* are out of the question.

There are many homes with hand-painted signs that say SE VENDE TORTILLAS, and we can buy four hot, fresh tortillas for one quetzal. That's like, 12 cents. We are allowed to eat those. We can also eat choco-bananas, which are frozen bananas dipped in chocolate. For a few *centavos* more, we can add peanuts or sprinkles.

Down the road, past the coffin shops and *pacas*, which are the heaps of Goodwill-rejected clothes for cheap, past the *librerias*, where they sell school supplies, is the town square. There's a bustling market where avocados are sold for one quetzal, and a dingy white Catholic church where a mariachi band plays at mass. More fruit cups. Lots of coffee shops with ample WiFi.

C Squad is all together this month. I like being with everyone, but I want a month alone with my team. It's hard for Brazen Hearts to find time to bond with everyone around.

Actually, we've started to go by Brazen Butts.

Our host, Julie, suggested to my team that when Brazen Butts start hospital ministry, we should work in the sterilization room, because there's only one woman there and she works all day long cutting bandages and preparing instruments for surgery. The work is grueling because it's so repetitive.

Today isn't an official ministry day, but we went over to the hospital to... I don't know. Introduce ourselves, I guess. We went to the front desk and said hello to a nurse. We asked if there was anything we could help with, and he told us to go outside and around the back. So, we walked all the way along the building to a big open garage. There were a couple guys with greasy clothes fixing things. We said we were missionaries, and asked if we, six unfamiliar young American women, could help them.

One of them pointed to a contraption that looked like a VCR bolted to a coat rack. He said it was a broken x-ray machine. He said we should fix it and then he left us alone in the garage.

Obviously, we couldn't fix it.

When we appeared again, we asked him for another job, and he pointed to two upside-down metal carts. He said that their wheels were coming loose, so we tightened and oiled them and flipped the carts back over.

We went back inside the hospital, and a receptionist said we could walk around and say hello to people. There weren't private rooms in this part of the hospital, just rows and rows of beds.

We picked an aisle to walk down and met a girl named Sandra, who told us she was 12 years old and had been hit by a car on December 27. She had been in the hospital ever since, and she was bored. We prayed with her, but then we sat on her bed and just chatted for a long time.

So today, six strangers showed up at a hospital and asked if there's anything they can do to help. Instead of being turned away, they are asked to repair an x-ray machine and metal carts, and then talk to all the patients. I can't *imagine* that happening in the States.

February 8
Santa Cruz del Quiché, Guatemala
Several of us went to the supermarket in downtown Quiché, which is called Despensa Familiar and is owned by Walmart. We had to shop for 44 people.

We bought 40 boxes of cereal.

That's 32,000 grams of cereal.

That's 70 pounds of cereal.

It was hard to walk back with the bags, so we are going to start borrowing shopping carts to get everything back home. The store is letting us do this as long as Nicole leaves her driver's license as collateral.

So far, we haven't been able to buy quite enough food on our budget. It's enough to not be hungry, but not enough to be full.

February 9
Santa Cruz del Quiché, Guatemala
We worked in the sterilization room for the first time today. The woman there is named Maria. She works all day folding gauze into parcels and wrapping stool sample bottles in stiff paper.

When we found the room, Maria opened the door and smiled at us. She made us put on scrubs in a locker room. She made us put on hairnets and face masks.

She did not give us gloves.

I enjoyed the simplicity of it, and the time it afforded for conversation. No strangers to approach and pray over, just my team and Maria. Maria was cute and giggly and we could not understand her at all, except for Nicole, who giggled back. Maria told us that she would make us tamales sometime and we could eat them (probably in the sterilization room).

The conversation moved to the topic of blood moons. Kori was explaining that there is a suspiciously high number of them this year and that it means the world is about to end, or something.

I try not to scoff when people get talking about that kind of thing, but Christians have sensed an imminent apocalypse for two millennia now, so excuse me if I'm skeptical.

A lot of people have started getting sick this month. This town is nearly 7000 feet above sea level, so maybe it's the altitude or the street food. Or maybe it's... you know, the devil.

February 12
Santa Cruz del Quiché, Guatemala
I bought a burger at Hamburguesa Mundo. It tasted great and I didn't feel sick.

I've also been eating a lot of choco-bananas and tortillas.

February 14
Santa Cruz del Quiché, Guatemala

The 11 men celebrated Valentine's Day by treating all 33 of us women like royalty today. They bought yogurt and made us homemade granola for breakfast, which is out of budget. Tony gave us dictator-themed cards that said things like "You're the Kim Jong-Illest" and "Be Mein." Mine says, "Leon Trotsky thinks you're hotsky!"

They did our chores. They made us a fancy dinner, set the table with real silverware and plates, and escorted us one by one to our seats. Since there are more women than men, they had to run back to get another one of us once we'd been seated. We ate chocolate, and bread with oil and vinegar.

They gave us each a red rose.

Jayce took photos of all of us with any friend combinations we wanted.

They put on a show for us. Daniel, Tony, and Jayce did a very repetitive dance routine to Cascada's "Every Time We Touch." Cody used to be a gymnast, and we all chanted, "STUNTS! STUNTS! STUNTS! STUNTS!" as he did backflips.

Then there was a magic show.

"Who likes animals?" shouted Tony. All the ladies, high on chocolate and soda and salad, raised our hands and screamed.

"Who likes pink?"

We screamed again.

"Who likes pink animals?"

Stacie and I lost our shit.

Tony closed his eyes and spun around and opened them and he was sort of pointing at me. He approached, did a magical gesture, and rummaged around in a towel, producing a *live*, neon pink chick. I shrieked and threw my head back in laughter.

"Thank you?!" I said, half delighted that I'd been given a present, and half horrified that someone had gone out and spent a quetzal on a creature that was doomed to die in my hands. In the markets, they dump hundreds of chicks into vats of dye as Easter approaches. A chick in any color costs one quetzal. *Cheap, cheap.*

It's fucking cute: *it's a pink chick.* But I'm scared it won't last long and that will make two months in a row with a dead baby animal.

Anyway, I haven't enjoyed Valentine's Day like that since grade school when everyone gave each other cards and candy. The guys bombarded us with esteem all day long.

Racers aren't supposed to date each other on the mission field, so this didn't feel remotely transactional; I mean, they honored us for free. Their affection was guileless. That's the way people should love each other.

February 16
Santa Cruz del Quiché, Guatemala

I left the chick in a box over the weekend with Mucho Nacho tortilla chips because it's all we had to feed her. She was fine the whole time we were at Lake Atitlán, but tonight, she was struggling to breathe. I don't know if it was a he or a she, but I assumed she, because of the pink. We named her Princess Sophia.

Wendy and I found ourselves half-heartedly caring for her as she met her agonizing fate. We put her in our laps, on a napkin, using a blow dryer on the low setting to keep her warm, but her breath was shallow and fast. I was half indifferent, but half heartbroken. She was a gift to me. She was a living creature. She should not have been dyed pink as a novelty item. That's no way to celebrate Easter.

Even as we laughed at ourselves for it, we prayed over her.

"God," said Wendy, "we know this is just a little animal, but we pray for your peace to be over this bird anyway. Either heal her and let her be big and strong, or take her painlessly. We know you care about the little things too."

She died and we placed her in the garbage heap and laid our Valentine's Day roses over her grave.

February 18

Santa Cruz del Quiché, Guatemala

They told us we were going to a government-run preschool today to help the teachers, but when we showed up, we learned that the staff had been on strike for months and we *were* the teachers.

It was horrific. There were hundreds of children and maybe ten adults. I couldn't keep the hordes of kids from climbing all over me and playing with my hair. I'm sure I contracted lice.

I went into a dim classroom where the toddlers kept peeing their pants and there weren't any spare clothes. I felt sort of bad for them but I mostly was cold and tired. It was just a normal day where I did not have the energy to work, let alone work with children.

There was a rose in the courtyard by the playground, and my squad-mate Stacie told me it smelled sweet. I was grumpy but I sniffed it anyway. The rose made me think of the rose petal ice cream I ate at the Eiffel Tower thirteen years ago, the first time I went abroad, and all sorts of other luxuries I've experienced traveling.

And now I live in a tent and don't get enough food. I don't know when I'll see a piano again. C Squad is getting sick from parasites and altitude and bad food. We travel to amazing places and spend all our time looking for the mundane. We didn't come here to tour. We came to pray for strangers in dirty hospitals and burn garbage. I don't control how I spend my days, but I know they will all be spent with other fine people who have uprooted themselves and surrendered control as well. I have never traveled like this before. I have never lived like this before.

I'm surprised that the hardships I see don't shock me and break my heart. Should they? It almost feels condescending, to try to get upset about other people's lives when I don't know them, so I'm not forcing those broken feelings. But there's a lot of talk about "being broken for the world," so I feel left out from that.

It's just that life is life here too, and roses smell sweet here too.

Leave It All

February 20
Santa Cruz del Quiché, Guatemala
C Squad is ill.

Half of us have been reduced to sleeping and barfing the days away. Ministry has dwindled. We weed patches of grass, kick soccer balls around, and go to the hospital now and then to pray for patients. Several of us have become patients ourselves. People were getting especially sick after visiting that preschool from hell, so we've abandoned it, to my relief.

We've been ignoring the food rules, and the squad leaders tattled on us to the World Race staff back in Georgia. They told us that seriously, we cannot eat any more Hamburguesa Mundo. They're cracking down on fruit cups too.

Tonight we're having macaroni and cheese with hot dogs. Andrea and Bre are watching *Juno*, Nathan is asleep with a book next to him and his headphones in, and Wendy and Courtney are passed out. Streamers from Valentine's Day hang limply from the ceiling and a cool breeze is about to upset the white awning. The dinner crew is starting to boil water.

Living in community is excellent because it yields scenes like this. It also sucks because there's no way out.

February 26
Antigua, Guatemala
We returned to Antigua today. We have a few days here before going to El Salvador. C Squad had its own chicken bus again. I was in the back row on the right and Tony was on the left.

As we entered Antigua after three or four hours, a short man jumped up on the back of the moving bus. I was confused. I watched him hold on and maneuver around the door, opening it and climbing into the center aisle. None of us in the back knew enough Spanish to tell him to get out, so we just said, "*No gracias, no gracias.*"

My mandolin, which had been propped against the door, started to fall out and the man caught it with his leg. I snatched it back and he jumped off.

Someone informed us that it's normal; people often board moving buses to sell fruits and vegetables.

What the hell?

February 27

Antigua, Guatemala

I used to wake up in the suburban house I grew up in and shower in a bathroom with heated floors and eat an everything bagel with cream cheese.

Now, I wake up in an airy Guatemalan hostel and have two rounds of explosive diarrhea in the bathroom under the crumbling stairs before putting on my only dress and enjoying a cup of coffee.

I don't want to be around people right now with their complaining and claustrophobia and internet-hogging. I want to be free to go wherever I want without a buddy. I want to not worry about whether my food will hurt me. I want my teammates to be healthy. I want to go out for drinks with Kori. I want to hang out with Tony. I want to be a tourist and I want WiFi that doesn't fail.

But I also want nothing and I want everyone to be impressed by how content I can be when I don't have those things.

COUNTRY 3:
EL SALVADOR

In which I hide in a laundry room
to escape working, sweat a lot,
and reach the end of my rope.

March 3
La Libertad, El Salvador
It was supposed to take five hours to get to El Salvador, but it took 10. The buses went to the wrong border and had to backtrack. Also, the meat pies we bought for breakfast had green mold so we couldn't eat them.

El Salvador looks like America because there are wide roads and fast food chains and they're on the dollar. But there are geckos and none of the place names are familiar, so we must still be gone.

We're staying in an orphanage. We're with team All Out, whose personnel has shifted a little and now includes Tony. Team changes like that happen all the time. I'm surprised Butts has been together this long. I bet we'll change after this month. Maybe they keep us together because we squabble sometimes and we're supposed to learn to invest in each other.

El Tunco is a cute surfing community a mile down the road, but we are locked in the orphanage all day. We'll help care for the fifty or so children who live here, and cook and clean and teach in the school next door.

But the main thing about this place is that it's hot. It is *so* hot. Think of all the metaphors in books about people traveling to tropical countries: the jungle critter on your chest, the hot tub dumped over your head, being swaddled in black leather in the sun... whatever. That's this. I don't know how hot it is because there is no internet to check, but it is too hot to function.

March 4
La Libertad, El Salvador
I'm scared.

We're supposed to wake up at 5:00 in the morning and work until dinnertime. I'm trying to negotiate that with Alma, our ministry host. I'm losing steam as a leader and I don't want to be locked up with kids this month in this heat.

Okay. Bedtime is good. I can take a shower, be alone in the dark, and put my headphones in.

I'll be not dismayed, for You are my God... I'll be disoriented, but I know that You know where I am... I can't handle it... You made this world... but You made it too hot.

I just have to smile at the kids, be a decisive leader, stay hydrated, call my family, talk to people, listen to people, work hard, write my blogs, read my Bible...

March 6
La Libertad, El Salvador

The orphanage has several buildings. There's the dining hall, where we have our coffee and meals, and where we keep our drinking water. There's the school, or the *colegio*. There's the chain-link cages of chickens on the hill, whose weekly slaughter brings in the money to feed the kids. There's the baby house for the infants and toddlers, which is where Cody, Jacob, and Tony stay. Brazen Butts and All Out's women stay in the girls' house in the back of the property, near an ever-burning fire over which an old woman sits cooking beans. We're in a room with too many rickety bunk beds. We're too big for them and we've already broken two or three of the frames.

My favorite place here is the lavandería. The lights don't work, there are six washers and dryers and none of those work either, and there's a *pila* full of water and cool tile floors. I always volunteer to do people's laundry. I take my time and get water all over myself and then doze on the tile floor and justify my slacking by playing Christian podcasts.

This is how a day goes here:

4:30: Hit the snooze button.

4:55: Get out of bed, put on clothes, and go to wake up the children.

5:00: Help the kids get ready for school and clean their common spaces.

5:45: Sweep and mop our own room to keep the ants out.

6:00: Go to the dining hall for coffee and cookies (Choco-Risas this month). It's already starting to get too hot for coffee, but I drink it anyway. Slice sour green mangoes and put them in sandwich bags for the *tienda* at the *colegio*, where they are sprinkled with chili flakes and sold for a quarter each.

6:30: Eat breakfast, which is probably rice and beans. Sometimes there's a black garbage bag full of doughnuts that are good once the ants are picked off.

7:30: Work in the school on the property, assisting in classrooms and wondering how to say, "Get off the table," or, "Don't kick his head," in Spanish. Mix and lay concrete by hand to make a sport court. Care for infants. Work in the kitchen.

10:30: Have a water break and snack from the tienda, like fried yuca, a quesadilla, or a frozen Gatorade.

12:30: Lunch time! Rice, beans, vegetables, and mystery meat. Hot sauce.

1:00: Siesta! Read a book or hang out with teammates if possible. More likely, pass out in front of the fan.

This is the time of day to flee to the shower. In my stink and sweat and stickiness, I peel off my clothes and enjoy the sort-of relief of the sort-of cold water, which I need pliers to turn on. Eat a blue raspberry bon-bon with gum in the middle and when the bon-bon's gone, get out of the shower. Get out and study my body. I don't know if I'm gaining or losing weight here, but what I am doing is tanning. There are actually *lines* on these Scandinavian shoulders. This is the only time of day I see my reflection.

2:00: Back to work. We may also help the kids with their homework and start on dinner.

5:00: Go to El Tunco to swim before dinner. No matter how hot and hard the days are, we have this to look forward to.

6:30: Dinner: more rice, more beans, more meat, more hot sauce.

7:00: Have team time.

8:30: Have another shower.

8:45: Adjust the fan to get a lot of air flow but not all of it, because I must share it with my teammates.

9:00: Sleep.

12:00: Wake up sweating. Consider moving to the tile floor which is cool, but crawling with ants. Fall asleep deciding.

March 7
La Libertad, El Salvador

Californian missionaries visited the orphanage today. They're in the country for two weeks and only a day here in La Libertad. They were eager to help us with our work and marginally less competent at speaking Spanish and mixing cement. They were cute and their ponytails were smooth and the neon piping on their running shorts was clean, signifying that *they* hadn't spent the year washing their clothes by hand.

All this made me feel great because I felt superior to them. Maybe we are sunburned, pissy slobs, but that's because we're spending nearly a *year* doing this shit. Can those Californians backpack like us? Probably not! We are badasses and they're just tourists. We've surrendered to Jesus and they're just in the shallow end.

We're special. *We're* called. Knowing that we're called (and they're not) makes me want to love these kids more. Sort of.

I guess that's pretty fucked up.

In addition to managing four KFCs, Tony says that he was a spy, that he spent time "on the protest circuit," and that he triple-majored in college. He also says he was ranked 32nd in the nation for Warhammer, some nerd game where you paint dragon dolls and make them fight.

He said he was happy playing but when he quit, he found joy.

But he still misses Warhammer because he no longer has a way to prove he's better than others.

That's an ugly truth about him. It's particularly ugly because it resonates with me. I wish I had a piano not only because I miss playing, but because I'm good at it. I wish someone would ask what my GPA was.

I wish there was *some* way to prove I'm better than most people at a lot of things because I'm not good at being a missionary.

Tony and Jacob and Cody spend their spare time in Baby Haus where the infants are stored. All the infants do is pee and cling to the guys' feet at the end of the work day. The guys are great with them. They give them rides on their shoulders and dance with them on their feet. If a kid hopped on my feet at the end of the day, I'd tell it, "I'm off-duty. *No mas.*"

God, what would You say to me? You would say that it's okay to not be inclined to this kind of work, but to do it anyway, see You there anyway. You don't want us to be ashamed of our passions, but we must not shirk our responsibilities.

March 8
La Libertad, El Salvador

Kori told me that I was acting arrogant because I said I didn't taste sour milk in a piece of cake but she did. Of course, it wasn't what I said, but the *way* I said it.

And we were all talking about how lice target blondes, and I half-joked that she was safe because her hair was only dyed blonde, and she was offended by that too. It wasn't funny, but it wasn't offensive. I don't know whether to be contrite or indignant.

I hate being called arrogant.

I miss my American life.

Everything's getting ruined, from my clothes to my feet to my composure. I'm going nuts. A good day is a day I can eat cookies alone in front of a fan without a licey head rubbing on mine.

It's only been three months. What about Africa. What about Asia. I'm not "broken for the world," like a good missionary should be. I'm just plain broken.

March 9
La Libertad, El Salvador

I left my Nook, external hard drive, and blue raspberry bon-bons on a top bunk in our room. The window was open.

Now I don't have a Nook, external hard drive, or blue raspberry bon-bons.

Tony thinks it's funny but I'm sad.

At least I still have my Bible, journal, iPhone, and MacBook Pro.

March 10
La Libertad, El Salvador

Diarrhea and intermittent stomach pains. Is it the beans? Or Satan?

Sick in bed.

I miss everything. I don't have my people, my home, my pride, my Nook, my food, my comfort, my privacy, my health, my talents. I live in an orphanage doing awful things like babysitting and frying pork rinds in hot oil. I don't give a shit about mission work.

It's the third month of the Race, and I'm hitting a wall.

I used to be excited about traveling the world and being the hands and feet of Jesus, but now I'd rather cling to vestiges of my old life. I keep thinking of home. I miss trees. I dream of cuddling with my vaccinated dogs, drinking tap water, and flushing toilet paper. I'm tired of finding ants in the hairy pork fat we eat. I'm tired of palm trees. I'm tired of not knowing Spanish. I'm tired of wondering if what I just ate will make me sick. I'm tired of filtering all my drinking water. I'm tired of rice, Gatorade, and Imodium.

And you know what else?

I'm tired of my life revolving around others.

My life always revolved around me. My parents nurtured me till I was old enough to go to school, where people worked to make me smart and successful and ready for college, where I studied in a bubble of campus housing and meal plans, all engineered for my comfort and success.

Now, no one I'm serving cares if what I do for them will beef up my resume or let me self-actualize. I do what I'm told and I take care of my team and my life is not my own. The Bible says our lives aren't our own, but I've always been cushioned from that truth. Now I'm not, and I can't handle it, and I'm *stuck*. I'm stuck in this lifestyle until November.

I can't make it to November by toughing it out and daydreaming of home. I have to adapt. We all do.

And we will. But in the meantime, all I can do is roll my eyes and ask myself over and over: *Why am I doing this?*

There has to be a great reason. Maybe it was once for the adventure, but that's not enough anymore.

And it can't be "for the kids." I don't even like kids.

And it can't be "for the world." That is abstract and exhausting.

Maybe I am here because I want to know the God who made me. In these 11 months of adventure and service, I want to encounter the Instigator and Fulfillment of reality like never before.

I can't think of anything else quite as compelling. That has to be it.

March 11
La Libertad, El Salvador

Our toilet paper is this wide:

From here *   * to here.

Just that wide.

I'm sick in bed again, and all I can think of is going back. I keep fantasizing about what it will be like to leave the Race.

I imagine that C Squad will fly into Los Angeles, and I'll say my goodbyes.

I'll fly to Seattle, *alone*.

I will see Mount Rainier through the clouds. If it's clear, the entire Cascade Range will stretch before me and then on the left, I'll see lights, and cars, and islands, and forests, and the rugged, rainy Olympics. And then my ears will pop and I'll sit still until the plane lands on familiar ground.

I won't rush to get off the plane. I'll sit and wait my turn. I won't turn my phone on right away.

When it's time, I'll take my bag out from under my seat and slowly savor the final steps of wild pilgrimage. Maybe my hips will slide between the seats easier; maybe not.

I'll step into the Sea-Tac terminal and turn my phone on and text Mom and Dad: "I'm here."

I will walk slowly through that airport. I'll stop right before exiting the terminal. I'll pause and consider my torn, hot-weather, Asian clothes. And then without thinking of much anything else I'll walk out and see my parents and siblings.

I will cry and embrace them. We'll go to baggage claim and David will insist on carrying my ragged red backpack, smothered with patches and grime. Mom won't let go of me. Dad will offer to take us out to dinner.

But we'll all just go home. The dogs will jump on me. I'll see the spot in the living room cleared for the Christmas tree. I'll see the big refrigerator and open the doors and see all the food.

I'll put my backpack on one last time, and my daypack, and my mandolin, and go upstairs to my childhood bedroom… and set it all down.

The Bible says not to worry about what we'll eat or wear or do but I am always worried about all those things. And I'm worried something will happen to my family, and I'm worried I'll get sick, and I'm worried these kids here aren't going to be okay, and I'm worried about what the next eight months of this trip are going to be like.

Plus, *we are forced to kill chickens on Fridays and the nasty children have some worrying tendencies.* They act like it's a party. They stick the birds down milk jugs and slit their throats and let the next victims smell the blood of the ones who went before. They pluck the feathers and throw them at each other. They chop off the feet and scratch each other.

I've started to "feel a little sick" or "want time in the Word" on Friday afternoons.

And you know what the hell else, we haven't been able to get *drinking water*.

We keep going through the big filtered jugs too fast, so in between deliveries, Jacob and I have been using our emergency water filters. We wore them out in a day, but we keep using them, eking warm tap water into the jugs way slower than our teams drink it. It takes so long, it's become one of the daily ministries, standing in the kitchen with Irene and the sugar bowls and the flying chicharrón grease and the hot, sweet, corny scent of tortillas, squeezing the worn-out filter.

March 12
La Libertad, El Salvador
Last night, when the heat of the day was still pressing on our shoulders, Kelsey led Brazen Butts to the basketball court at the school. She wanted to relax and listen to music.

As I spread out on a concrete step, I felt a raindrop.

A giant, cold raindrop.

I sat up and looked at my team.

"But where are the clouds?" I asked.

"The whole *sky* is clouds!" said Nicole.

"You guys, it's going to rain!" said Kelsey.

We lay on the cement steps, still warm from the day, and looked to the heavens in delight as the deluge came. The singer kept repeating, "It's all gonna be okay, it's all gonna be okay."

The rain fell harder and harder. It unlocked a smell unique to the geographical coordinates of this orphanage: a spicy, earthy funk with notes of concrete and garbage. I will never forget that smell.

The rain fell harder still, until I started getting legitimately wet and cold for the first time all month. It rooted me here, with these people, on the sport court in the dark.

I lay there, staring at the sky with my mouth open (you don't need to filter rainwater) and Jesus told me that He'd been planning that rain for a long time, and that everything *would* be okay, and that He knew exactly what we needed and He was caring for us.

We listened to three long songs and the rain stopped just when they did.

March 13
La Libertad, El Salvador
I saw a scorpion behind the toilet today. I'm sick of Central America again.

March 16
La Libertad, El Salvador
Tonight in the shower, the water was so cold, it gave me goosebumps! They replaced the drowsy old shower heads with PVC pipes, and the water gushes out and it's not comfortable to stand under, which is wonderful.

It feels good to feel like I'm getting used to this. Maybe I'm not, maybe it's just a cloudy day and we have different water pressure, but when I get cold in this country, or know which *tienda* has Fresca, it feels good. Good-ish.

I hear God telling me to relish the specific life I have today, even if I don't like most of it. A kid slobbered on my water bottle, and then I forgot it at the beach. I wear the same things all the time because of the heat. My clothes are getting destroyed fast because I wash them by hand and I'm not good at it. I sit in the laundry room because it is cool and dark and tiled.

My life will not always be like this. I ought to be embracing this season of weakness, because there is texture to it. God does not want me to quit.

March 18
La Libertad, El Salvador
Irene, the cook, has a six-year-old daughter named Fanny, and Nicole says Fanny is exactly like her. They take selfies and Fanny gets in her face and is obnoxious, but Nicole just laughs and kisses her. It's beautiful but I don't have the energy to be that nice to Fanny myself.

March 21
La Libertad, El Salvador
My underwear is rubbing me wrong and it hurts. My butt crack is chafing. *Jesus, in Your mighty name, I claim complete healing over my butt.*

Jacob and I lugged a huge pot of tomatoes in water to the next village to visit a woman who had a meat grinder. There were other people there with their own pots who wanted to grind things, so Jacob and I waited a while. We sat under a tin roof in dirty white plastic chairs. An out-of-date calendar fluttered on the chipped blue walls, which had been painted many times over. Geckos scuttled around.

Jacob told me that culture shock often doesn't set in until after three months in a place.

"At first, people are usually pretty good at adjusting to a new environment, because it's so fresh and exciting," he said. "But once it doesn't feel like an adventure anymore, it gets harder and that's when you get people who want to go home."

Maybe that's what has been happening to me.

Leave It All

March 23
La Libertad, El Salvador
I've been telling the kids all month that my name is "Chelsea, like the football club," so they always pitch two teams and ask my favorite: "Chelsea or Manchester? Barcelona or Madrid?"

I think Barcelona is the correct answer with this crowd, so I say that. I think they're also Manchester fans, I suggested they call me "Man-Chelsea," and they loved that.

March 26
La Libertad, El Salvador
A Salvadoran missionary named Juan came and talked to our team today and made me more okay with being a missionary. We sat in a classroom after the school day was over.

Juan said, "I work for the gospel here in my country, but they ignore me. I don't know why the people here listen to gringos but ignore us, but that is how God is working right now and so as long as the gospel is preached, I am happy."

I wonder what we're doing here, in another country we don't understand, whose language we haven't had the decency to learn, and that answers that a little.

He said, "You can show people Jesus in a way that's new, that they've never seen before. Not because you have a superior culture, but simply because you're different and people notice that you have left your life to come here."

He said, "Don't go to heaven with just your family, though that'd be enough. Take a country with you." He also said, "Trust in God. God will give you the desires of your heart."

It's bedtime, but before I sleep I must say: I should have acted out when I had the chance.

I got no action at Vassar. I was so good at Vassar. I think of Vassar in the springtime, when everyone smoked hookah on the quad and flirted in secondhand sundresses they could have bought new, riding the end of adolescence by finding pleasure and problems in the most creative places.

For four years, I walked myself home at night, passing parties I didn't crash, pot I never smoked, hookups I never wanted or understood how to get. I never even tried any of that because I fell into the Vassar Christian Fellowship. I fell into community. I fell into a family that was so loving, so full of life, so close to heaven, so vocal about dispersing darkness, so passionate about worship, so vulnerable, so empowering, so spontaneous, so *funny*, that I didn't get around to casual sex or binge drinking. I wouldn't be here if those people hadn't shown me how big life with Jesus can be... but *still*, even though I *know better*, I wish I could go back and fall in the pursuit of cheap, dirty pleasure.

I know it's futile.

I know it's fake.

I know it's small.

But I never *did* it.

I never came honestly to the conclusion of how that shit never satisfies. It wouldn't have felt good for long, but it would've felt good. Now I wish I could hook up with someone I don't care about and get drunk and try some weird drug and be too loud. I don't want to be disciplined or wise at all—and guess what? I don't even think those appetites are evil. I think it's fine to feel this way. I think they are tactile and visceral and sensual, and the sensual world this month holds so few instances of physical respite.

But because I'm on a *mission trip*, everything is about the eternal. We're always praying toward heaven and toward what will be someday, but I'm not *interested* in the eternal. I'm interested in finding a way to cool my body down and not be so tired all the time. These days are marked with the blood of chickens, and ant-studded glazed doughnuts in black garbage bags, and hairy pig fat, and grubby kids, and crayons, and petty arguments, and the condensation of Fresca cans on the back of our necks, and mundane chores carried out in broken Spanish, and mixing cement by hand on the blacktop, and *living* for the occasional, air-conditioned grocery story run. We are literally locked in this house and there are bars on the windows and doors, and I do not want a cloister. I want *out*.

And yet... I am *still here*.

March 27
La Libertad, El Salvador

A change in continent is imminent. I am thrilled about it, but weirdly, a little sad to leave.

When we leave for Europe we are going to have team changes, and I won't be a leader anymore. My pride hurt a little bit when Jeff, one of the squad leaders, called me and said that, but only for an instant. No team leader stays a leader the whole time, and I'm sick of it anyway.

I think maybe this has been a great month. I wouldn't say I crushed it, but I feel like God's proud of me anyway. I think it has mattered.

March 29
La Libertad, El Salvador

Tomorrow, we drive to San Salvador. We'll fly to Houston, then to Washington, D.C., then Istanbul, then Tirana, Albania. From Tirana, we'll bus east across Macedonia and into Bulgaria.

They haven't told us how long it will take. This time, I'm not going to ask.

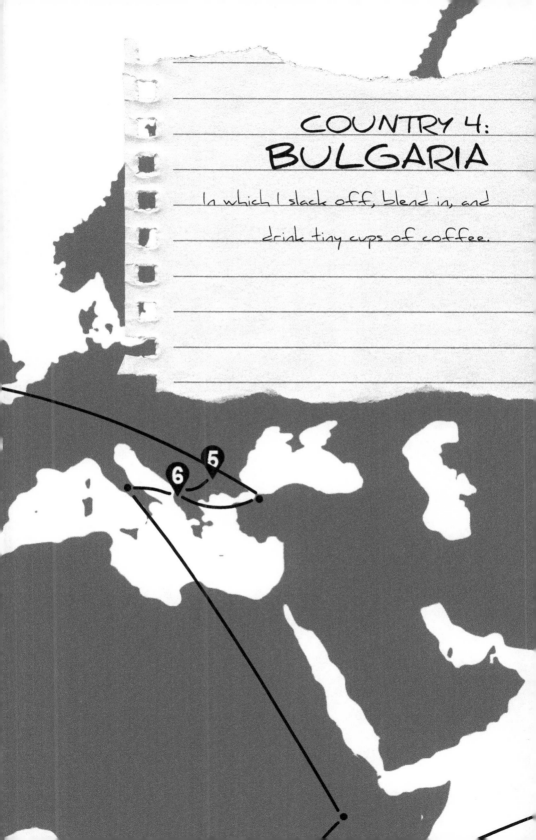

COUNTRY 4:
BULGARIA

In which I slack off, blend in, and

drink tiny cups of coffee.

March 31
Flight from San Salvador, El Salvador to Houston, Texas, USA

I have a new team: Arden, Daniel, Matthew (whose name has morphed to Mateo after three months in Central America), Deborah, Kori, and Nicole. This is going to be fun group. We named ourselves Deep Roots and have already shortened it to Doots.

I'm *so* happy to be on a plane. The half-filled cups of coffee, the movies, the crappy food for purchase: it's homey.

Flight from Houston, Texas to Washington, D.C., USA

The customs guy in Texas said, "Welcome home." But I wasn't going home, I was leaving all over again.

After being in D.C. for a couple minutes, I will be gone for eight months. What if I hate it? What if every month is like El Salvador? I'm supposed to believe it'll be okay, but that's not guaranteed, no one guaranteed that. I could hate the rest of this trip. That's possible.

This is how I used to feel on roller coasters, back when I was afraid of them: we're clicking up, up, up, up, and it's too late to turn back, and it'll be what it'll be, we'll just have to go down…

Istanbul, Turkey

This is a busy airport. I haven't slept. I don't know how long we've been traveling. It's 4:00 p.m.

Kori, Carly, and I went to the makeup section of a duty-free store and Kori was mistaken for a massage therapist by two Cretan women because they saw her rubbing my back while I slumped in a makeup chair and snuck moisturizer from sample tubes. Kori said she wasn't a therapist, but she rubbed their backs anyway.

Leave It All

April 1
Tirana, Albania

The bus that was going to take us from Albania to Bulgaria tonight didn't show up. It's coming at 7:00 tomorrow morning instead. This is *great* news, because it means we'll spend the night in the airport on the floor of a closed restaurant instead of on a bus. I haven't slept since leaving El Salvador.

Albanian is not like Spanish. I cannot understand a word. I can't even *guess* what they're saying.

April 2
Tirana, Albania

I slept well and woke up at 4:43 a.m. in Europe feeling delightedly cosmopolitan.

I stretched and assembled my hair into what I assumed was a sexy topknot and put on my flannel and went to a bar, feeling refreshed and empowered. I found words on the menu I understood.

I said, "Brioche. Espresso," and they appeared before me as I put down some lekë and enjoyed the first dawn of approximately 60 in Eastern Europe. A glance at my reflection in the espresso machine revealed that my topknot was not sexy.

The bus didn't pick us up at 7:00. It will come at 7:00 in the *evening* instead.

Rather than wait in the airport any longer, we took our luggage and bused into downtown Tirana to kill 12 hours. Doots ate pizza and played Uno at a coffee shop. We were so tired, we really just took turns putting the cards on the table and picking them up again. The coffee was thick and dark and came in tiny cups.

Eventually we reunited with the rest of the squad on a grimy side street and put our bags in a big pile and napped on top of them for a few hours. Businessmen kept turning off the main road to our street and peeing on a nearby concrete wall.

April 3
The bus that's been blasting techno music all night, entering Bulgaria
This will be a 14-hour bus ride.

We left at 7:00 p.m. and drove east, entering Macedonia at 3:00 a.m. I set foot on Macedonian earth for a pay-to-use squatty potty, the kind of toilet that's a hole in the floor.

We entered Bulgaria at 6:00 a.m.

The sun is now coming up. I see mountains with snow on them, and pine trees and dreary stone houses.

I see a tall, dark-haired woman walking by an old concrete wall. She wears a long, gray sweater and the wall wears graffiti. Behind the wall is a house covered in pink flowers.

Sofia, Bulgaria
We're in Sofia, at our ministry site: an American family's apartment. The 22-year-old son, Timmy, met us at the station and we took a metro to his home. Timmy and his parents Stan and Mary are our hosts. Stan is the pastor of an international church and we're going to be working with the refugees who attend. But that will only be a few hours a week, so I don't know what else we'll do.

Getting from La Libertad, El Salvador to Sofia, Bulgaria ended up taking 76 hours.

April 4
Sofia, Bulgaria
I love Team Doots.

I love having WiFi at home.

I love breathing cool air.

I love the architecture of Sofia.

I already feel how easy it is to ignore God now that I'm comfortable. This is a beautiful European capital, where the Bible stories that shaped me are safely preserved in mosaics in dark, luminous cathedrals, where our ministry schedule is light and easy, where I look like the locals, and where I can go to H&M whenever I want. I do not want to forget God. God has brought me here. God is God here, too.

Life was so different one week ago.

April 7
Sofia, Bulgaria

This morning, we are sitting at the kitchen table. We are listening to worship music and praying quietly.

Later, since we have no ministry scheduled, we'll do A.T.L., which stands for "Ask the Lord." It's when we pray and listen to God and then go do whatever the Spirit prompts us to do.

A.T.L. is usually simple and beautiful. Once, in Guatemala, Kelsey had a vision of a woman selling flowers, so we looked for the woman all day and finally saw her as we were going home. She had a big flower stand on the sidewalk and Kelsey recognized her from her vision. We said hello and prayed for her and chatted. If God hadn't told us to look for that connection, it would not have happened.

Yesterday, we went to a park and felt led to play music (Arden had his guitar and I had my mandolin) near some teenagers, and then it turned into a jam session with them, and they installed the Bulgarian keyboard on my iPhone, and now I have three new Facebook friends.

Mostly, it's this: I pray, God takes me out of my comfort zone, and I connect with strangers in simple, kind ways. I've only seen good come from it.

But I get skeptical of it anyway. Praying? Okay. Listening to God? Okay. Getting words and visions and encouragements to share? Okay… but still, I fear it. I'm afraid of rejection. I'm afraid of being an annoying weirdo. I don't want people to feel threatened by my religion. I don't want people to dislike me.

Country 4: Bulgaria

April 8

Sofia, Bulgaria

A Liberian refugee named Kirby took us to see *Captain America 2*.

I don't like superhero movies, and the power went out in the theatre right at the climax, but it was nice to sit in squishy chairs and zone out for a bit.

Plus, I realized something. In the movie, there's a part where Captain America says that he just wants to do the right thing.

I'm not like Captain America. I don't just want to do the right thing. I want to do the easy thing. I just spent three months doing the right thing by helping strangers and holding kids and praying a lot, and it kind of sucked. It's worn me out and it hasn't been that rewarding. I hope that what we're doing here in Bulgaria is good and true, but I like this month so much because it's so easy, and I'm so comfortable, and we do so little ministry, and I want it to stay that way. It's not a nice fact that I feel this way. But it's a fact.

April 11

Borovci, Bulgaria

We've left Sofia to spend a week in Borovci, a Roma village in Montana near the Serbian border. Up here, there are rose farms. Grass grows over the train tracks. The station is falling apart. Mountains hem us in. There are shaggy dogs everywhere. Dreary, dreary houses and broken roads. The tulips are the reddest things I've ever seen.

We're at a home for men who have aged out of the orphanage system and lack professional skills. The program here trains them in things like carpentry and upholstery. There are only five living here now because a lot just graduated, and they're fun to hang out with. We painted a few ceilings, but otherwise, I don't know what we're supposed to be doing here. We play Monopoly and shoot hoops with the guys. When our team is alone, we take Buzzfeed quizzes and pick lice out of each other's hair.

At the center of Borovci, everyone just sits. Twice a day, at 10:30 and 2:00, everyone gathers at the cafe, sits on plastic chairs, and drinks sludgy coffee from little plastic cups. Everyone chats while the rain falls on the bricks. We wear sweaters but it's not too cold.

My heart hasn't been in the manual labor or the praying or the children this year. Maybe that makes me a bad missionary.

It's just that I see people sitting, just *sitting*, having coffee and being together, and there's a goodness there that can't be improved on. That's real life. Sitting with each other. That's what I love. Is *that* my ministry?

Sometimes I feel like the team weirdo. Sometimes I feel like I'm not Christian enough for mission work, if I'm finding God in cups of coffee.

April 13
Borovci, Bulgaria

We have been playing Poison Dart Frog a lot. If we make eye contact with someone and they pretend to shoot a blow dart, we have to fall over where we are and can't move until someone taps us and unfreezes us. It's kind of been interfering with ministry but it's really funny.

April 19
Sofia, Bulgaria

Our team theoretically works with refugees, but that's just three hours a week. We go to church on Sundays and occasionally do A.T.L., but that's about it. We hang out with Timmy and his friends. The other night, some of us went to a hookah bar and ordered apricot smoke. Another night, we saw traditional Bulgarian dancing and ate lots of potato dishes. And another night, we just had beers at some random people's apartment.

I'd be lying if I said I wanted more work.

April 20
Sofia, Bulgaria
Today is Easter.

Yesterday, on Holy Saturday, we went to a birthday party at an ale-house. The booths had beer taps at each table. We could fill our glasses whenever we wanted, and a meter attached to the tap kept track of how much we owed. It was so cheap and had so little alcohol, we filled our glasses over and over just to marvel at the bargain and our sobriety.

But then the bill came, and we realized the meter had been measuring how many *liters* of beer we had drunk, not the price per liter. That's how they get you in Bulgaria.

Late at night, we made our way to Nevsky Cathedral. It was chilly and raining. Men were chanting and wearing shiny robes at the church entrance, and a crowd was gathered around the spectacle, passing each other thin yellow candles.

At midnight, one of the clergy shouted through a scratchy speaker: "*Hristos vozkrese!*" Christ has risen!

"*Voistina vozkrese!*" shouted back the crowd. He is risen indeed!

Everyone started hugging and kissing each other and repeating the phrases.

The men in red and gold lit more fires and said things I didn't understand. We lit our own candles. Mine went out immediately and snapped in half. But Mateo's burned right onto his thumb. They say that the longer your candle burns, the more saintly you are.

Then, the crowd walked around the church three times and we went home with the light of Christ shining in our hearts.

(I only did two laps.)

April 21
Sofia, Bulgaria
They say to never, ever, ever stop following Jesus with your whole heart, like growing in faith is a steady upward trajectory. But it's not steady or linear. It's a spiral, weaving through doubt and faith

and distance and intimacy, despite and because of human effort and desire. Seasons of distance and skepticism precede and follow those of rapture and piety. Sometimes we remember God, and other times we forget and God calls us all over again. I have to believe God is God even when we forget God is God.

This month has been an easy month. I have been happy with my team and happy with this country. We haven't done a lot of work and I've liked that.

This month, I don't know if I've done *wrong* things, but I've certainly chosen easy things. I wonder if it has dulled my spirituality.

April 24
Sofia, Bulgaria

Tonight, I tried the doors of a Catholic cathedral on the way to get gelato, but it was locked and my team didn't want to go in anyway.

It's these times that make it feel like a waste, traveling all over the world without being allowed to wander alone and see the sights. I feel like I'm missing out on so much.

After no one helped me look for a way in, I gave the two leva I would have used to light a candle to a guitarist at the stairs down to the metro station.

April 25
Sofia, Bulgaria

Arden asked Team Doots if the Race makes us want to do long-term missions more or less. I said less, because I haven't loved any of our ministries yet and I don't feel called to missions anyway. It was weird to say that out loud. My heart is not breaking for the rest of the world, but I am walking the path of someone for whom it does. Is that good or bad?

COUNTRY 5:
ALBANIA

In which I make my bed, write a
poem, and wallow in pig poop.

April 28
Tirana, Albania
We had some time to tour the city today, so we went into a mosque.
I'd never been in one. It was beautiful. It wasn't oblong like a cathedral—it was all squares and circles. Botanical motifs wound up the
ceiling and words I didn't understand adorned the walls. There were
no pews. But Kori had to leave because it was making her feel sick.
She said she could feel a bad spirit in the place.

She's so sensitive to spiritual things. I'm not. I *like* other religions. Is there something wrong with me, that mosques don't make
me dry heave? Would I be a more devoted Christian if they did? Do
I have to be more like Kori, or are she and I just different?

We're all worshipping in a conference room attached to a cafe.
People are playing guitar and singing the same several worship
songs we've been singing for four months. I'm not feeling it. I'm sitting against the wall and writing in my journal instead. Everyone's
hands are up and they are weeping about how much they trust Jesus.
I feel isolated because I can't get to the place they all seem to be in.
I can't get on board. They are singing at nothing. They are singing
at the ceiling. Back in college, I used to dance and hop around in
worship, full of joy. What happened? Did I burn out? Did I study
too much? Why don't I do that anymore?

Yet here, as I compare myself to them, I also feel God whispering tenderly to me that I do not need to summon moods or perform
mental gymnastics to work myself into a state approximate to theirs.

I feel God telling me that my skepticism is not to be feared.

April 29
Tirana, Albania
Our Bulgaria hosts Stan and Mary sent an email to the World Race
administrators saying that Team Doots was awful last month. They
said that we crowded their space, didn't clean up, picked out our

lice on their furniture, dyed our hair in their sink, and didn't do any work. So, after dinner, Bobby, Sharon, and Hope called us together and read the laundry list of complaints.

They asked, "Which of these errors do you take responsibility for, and which do you not?"

Item by item, we worked through it. Overall, we should have been more considerate, and they should have been more communicative. It cast April in a different light and we grew closer to each other as we cried in disappointment and swore to do better next month.

Now, I'm sitting on the hostel roof, admiring the way distant towns float and glitter in the hills. I'm thankful for the hard night and I'm thankful that we get another month. I will try not to choose the easy things in May.

April 30
The bus to Lezhe, Albania

Oak is my third team. Arden is on it again, plus Jayce, Jason, Heidi, and Courtney. We chose the name because oaks are strong and powerful, and it's a short word.

Most of C Squad is staying at a camp on the outskirts of a town called Lezhe, near the coast. "Lezhe," if said wrong (and I don't know how to say it right), apparently sounds like a very bad word.

May 2
Lezhe, Albania

We can see the town of Lezhe from the rooftop deck of the main building. The river behind our property meanders toward its center. The town is unremarkable, but parts of it creep up on the big hill that looms behind it, and on top of the hill is a castle.

The summer camp is in yet another compound, of course. The buildings are spacious and airy, yellow on the outside and white on the inside. We sleep in rooms with white tile floors and heavy bunk beds and pilling blankets. Three women, two of whom are Muslim and one of whom is Catholic, cook all the meals. For breakfast we eat white bread, hard-boiled eggs, butter, cheese, and preserves. For lunch and dinner we eat a heap of pasta with white bread and cooked cabbage on the side. Sometimes, we get little sausages, and cucumber and tomato salad.

There's a bed and breakfast next door where we buy fast WiFi and cheap fries.

This month, our job will be to prepare the camp for the hordes of children it will host this summer. I am going to work hard and try not to suck so much this month.

May 4
Lezhe, Albania

My stomach's been hurting for a couple days. Back home, I don't think anything of stomach aches or sore throats, but out here, I'm always afraid of contracting some rare, deadly disease. I asked Arden, Kori, and Deborah to pray for me and I'm glad I did. Arden said that it was good of me to ask, that it takes bravery to do that kind of thing. I didn't want to ask for prayer for something so specific, because if it didn't work, then what?

They prayed for me, and they all had the sense that this wasn't indicative of a big problem, and that I shouldn't have any fear.

"I hear Jesus say three things," said Kori. "Imodium, water, and no more cabbage."

May 8
Lezhe, Albania

I haven't been eating the cabbage and my stomach is better. I didn't even go to the clinic.

We've been working a lot. We've been painting pig stalls white. We've been setting up the climbing wall and the obstacle course. We've been eating all the bread and pasta we can. We've been laughing a lot.

We've been listening to each other's favorite podcasts to pass time while we paint. We've been sleeping hard.

May 12
Lezhe, Albania

Everyone is starting to get worked up about our next continent shift.

"Oh, if we think these dinners of pasta and white bread are hard, wait till *Africa!*"

"If we think whitewashing is hard, wait till *Africa!*"

"If God's showing up here, wait till *Africa!*"

Daniel talked to everyone. He said something to the effect of, "Calm the fuck down about Africa." Except he didn't say "fuck."

We hold Africa in our minds as this otherworldly, inscrutable swirl of unprecedented chaos and glory, this mystical continent where the *really* hardcore missionaries go. All it does is psyche us out and makes us shortchange our experience of Albania.

May 17
Lezhe, Albania

"All My Clothes Are Nasty"
All my clothes are nasty, and that's not an understatement.
It started in Honduras and goes on without abatement.
Part of it's my fault, I know. How could I have foreseen
Just how rough the concrete is that scrubs our garments clean?
Now little holes are everywhere, each shirt and skirt and sock,
At least they're clean, I tell myself, sewing around the clock.
Yet ancient stains remain, and yellowed collars curl;
It's my perforated wardrobe that I haul around the world.
One day in Tirana, we were caught out in the rain.
The sweater I was wearing left an awe-inspiring stain.
Now my favorite denim shirt, the one for special days,
Has become an algae art project: well, I see it that way.

Now, as for shoes, I have to say, the worst is yet to come:
I fear the brownish pigsty grime has only yet begun.
My Chacos often give me blisters, not their usual love.
You can see my flip flops' soles from under and above.
My towel stinks, my blanket reeks, my coat's a fetor trap.
And just this very morning, my purple watch band snapped!
El Salvador left sand, sand, sand, sand, sand, sand, sand, sand, sand,
It's everywhere still: sand, sand, sand, sand, sand, sand, sand, sand, sand—
AND!
A part of me fears lice and ticks, if somewhere they may lurk:
No wonder socks fly off the line, in search of kinder work.
One shirt is stained with hair dye and what else, I can't recall.
And even if my clothes were new, I'd still be tired of them all.
That's just my clothes: don't get me started on the other stuff.
But it's okay, we're all this way, a little frayed and rough.
It's kind of fun to be a mess with forty other messes.
Though I love clothes and colors, that's not really what impresses.
Instead, go read your Bible and then give some stuff away,
'Cuz what is this "looking perfect" thing?
What is that, anyway?

May 21
Lezhe, Albania
Wake up. Make bed. Eat carbs. Work hard. Eat carbs. Work hard. Buy fries and beer. Laugh a lot. Get WiFi. Eat carbs. Unmake bed. Sleep.

May 22
Lezhe, Albania
At the beginning of the month, a couple people found a newborn, nearly-dead puppy in our dumpster and took it out and wrapped it

in a blanket and named it Tucker. I wished they hadn't. I didn't want to see a dog die.

But Tucker is alive! She has doubled in size. Her squeaks are louder. Her fur is growing. Her eyes have opened. Her belly is round and she can almost walk.

The credit for Tucker's survival goes entirely to a group of committed, loving squad-mates who have recognized hers as a life worth saving. They've logged sleepless nights and long days working during our breaks to keep Tucker fed and warm.

I'm finally taking the graveyard shift with her tonight. I haven't wanted to, because I like my sleep. I'll have to wake up every few hours to give her a bottle of milk and fill my Nalgene with hot water to keep her box warm. I also have to make her poop, which Bre told us we can do simply by stimulating her anus with a tissue.

We don't know what will come of Tucker, since we can't travel with her and no one here seems to want her. But even if it's inconvenient and unrealistic, it's worth it to try to save a life. It's the beautiful thing to do.

May 24
Lezhe, Albania

Last night around one in the morning, Wendy went to the bathroom, but she couldn't find the light switch, so she just went in the dark. When she went to wash her hands, the soap fell off the edge of the sink into the mop bucket. She crawled on her hands and knees to feel around for it, but she couldn't find it, so she went to the other end of the bathroom to use the soap there.

On the other side of the wall, Kori heard shuffling in the bathroom. She heard toilets flushing and sinks running and things banging and splashing. She sat up in her bunk and reached to jostle Nicole:

"Nicole, I need you to go to the bathroom with me!"

"Why, Kori?"

"There's definitely something in there! Seriously, there is something in the bathroom!"

She dragged Nicole out of bed and slowly approached the bathroom. In the darkness, they tried to see what was there.

All of a sudden, a black shadow appeared in the doorway and came toward them. Kori jumped and grabbed Nicole's arm and started yelling,

"In the name of Jesus, *back up*! Back up! We rebuke you in the name of Jesus! Who are you?!

"Guys?" Wendy whimpered, and then they recognized her and started laughing.

We've all been laughing all breakfast long about it.

I guess Wendy said something to the effect of, "Why would a demon flush a toilet?"

May 26
Lezhe, Albania

Five months down. Six months to go. I feel pretty good!

Did I just hit my wall in El Salvador? Was it just that one tough month? Will everything be easy from here on out? Have I hit my stride?

Today I live in Lezhe, Albania, and in one week I'll live in Lusaka, Zambia. That is so cool.

Our host found out about Tucker.

"*Oh*," he said in his sardonic British drone, "are you teaching it to swim?" Then he motioned to the river behind the property.

May 27
Lezhe, Albania

It's hard to believe, but C Squad's time in Europe is coming to an end. On Saturday, we have a long layover in Rome. On Sunday, we fly through Ethiopia and land in Zambia.

But before we get there, here are some things I've learned in Albania:

1. Make your bed.

At the start of the month, our host challenged us to be disciplined by keeping our areas neat and our beds made.

My first response to being charged with a task like this is usually, "What difference does it make? It's *my* bed, and I like it messy. You can't tell me what to do. You're not the boss of me. Are you saying you're the boss of me? Because I like my stuff messy, so stop trying to be the boss of me."

But then... I started making my bed. And I began to feel more respect. I don't know for what, exactly. Perhaps the bed. My property, others' property. I didn't expect it, but that single detail helped me care about other details in our daily work.

2. Work hard.

This month, I wanted to make a point of doing hard work well. Our ministry wasn't centered around people. Our job was to paint, plaster, weed, chop, organize, haul, take inventory, scrape, and rinse a summer camp into shape. I thought it would be hard to fall into the groove of working hard every day. I was afraid that I would get lazy and cut corners. So, my intention at the start of May was to work with integrity and be proactive about serving this camp—even if it meant working a little past the end time or waking up a little earlier than I preferred.

Well, it took a while to get used to manual labor all day. But at the end of the month, it feels good to know we were faithful with the tasks we were given.

We did more work than expected. Upon our arrival, we had to whitewash the pig farm, the front gate, the halls, the bedrooms, the meeting spaces, and the bathrooms. We had to repaint all the gates and grates, and clear a path through the bushes in the back. After a few days of working, it became clear that these jobs would get done before the month was halfway through, so we put plaster over cracks in the walls. We weeded.

We cleaned the pool and organized two warehouses and cleaned out thousands of empty ice cream containers and washed cars and set up an obstacle course and set routes on the rock wall and castrated and vaccinated pigs and sanded and stained doors and tiled a veranda.

3.   *God provides.*

I need to have all my money raised by the end of next month; that means I need $1595 more to reach my final deadline of $15,500. Sometimes I'm nervous that the money won't come in. But then I remember how Jesus said in the Sermon on the Mount that we shouldn't waste our time worrying about having what we need. Birds and flowers don't blog or have jobs and they're perfectly fine.

I'm also not nervous about asking other people for money anymore, so I'm going to right now: would you be open to giving to support my ministry in all these places? It's not that I'm great or that I know so much about being a missionary or anything. I'm actually sort of bad at it. But God is good, and God loves the world, and God has brought me to this trip and this work.

Would you be willing to be a part of my story (which is a chapter of God's) and give $10? $50? $100? $500? $1000? $1595?

May 29
Lezhe, Albania
Today in one word would be *shit.*

We were supposed to have a day off, because we are about to travel to oh, I don't know... *Africa*, and I was so excited to relax all day. But *instead*, our host George, who maybe wants to drown our dog, gathered us together and said that we needed to dig a channel behind the pig farm so the *years'* worth of pig shit would flow directly into the river instead of the sloppy field behind their enclosures. But that's where the pig shit *had* been, in the sloppy pig shit field, so we put on boots that were too short and too small and stood up to our knees in shit all day long on the one hot day of the month, shoveling and wheelbarrowing and sweating. There was so much liquid poop everywhere it wasn't even gross after a while, even though it was in between our toes and up and down our thighs.

I'm across from Nate at a table at the bed and breakfast now. We're not talking to each other. We're just sitting still, drinking the best beers of our lives. My eyes are so itchy and so sticky and crusty, I think if I close them, they'll get stuck that way. I'm so tired, a part of me is genuinely worried I won't wake up in the morning. I'm dead tired.

May 30
Lezhe, Albania
Tomorrow, to Italy and Ethiopia. Sunday, to Zambia. Not sure how long it will take.

I'm getting nervous about Africa.

May 31
The flight from Rome, Italy to Addis Ababa, Ethiopia
We had maybe ten hours in Rome. I don't have to say what it was like. It was like a movie. The rushing from Colosseum to Forum to Vatican to Trevi Fountain, the gluttonous pasta and wine lunches, the budgets neglected, just this once.

We ran up the Spanish Steps. We went into all the fancy designers, Prada, Armani, and everything else, just because they felt so strange. We stumbled upon *two* sumptuous weddings. One was taking place in a cathedral we poked our noses in. And the other was near the Forum. We saw the bride getting out of her limousine, and she looked upset, so we hid behind a stone wall and prayed for her.

And then, having force fed ourselves as much Rome as we could, we found ourselves on this plane, to a continent most of us know nothing about.

COUNTRY 6: ZAMBIA

In which I ask some questions about mission work, go to church all the time, and exit the mysterious, exclusive 10 Percent Club.

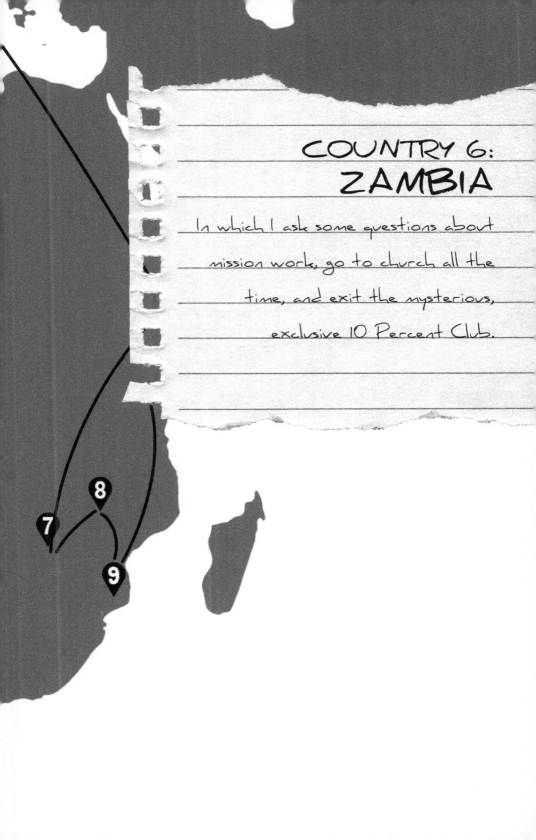

June 1
Addis Ababa, Ethiopia
This airport has dirty windows and dim light.

Harare, Zimbabwe
The plane to Lusaka has made an unannounced pit stop in Harare. Across the aisle, an Herbalife guy is trying to sell Kori vitamins.

Lusaka, Zambia
On the final descent, Shannon gave me one of her earbuds and put on "Africa" by Toto, which somehow I'd never heard. Maybe God wanted me to hear it for the first time when I was landing in Zambia.

A pastor named Kebby picked up Team Oak. We hadn't slept in 40 hours, but some of us sat in the bed of Kebby's truck on top of the baggage. The wind of a new hemisphere slapped us awake.

It was golden hour. The ground was red and the grass was green and the trees were brown. The land was flat like they say the Midwest is, and... what was the sky?

Blue. Blue and big. Blue like a poem. Blue like I could walk up and touch it. I could see the seam between the sky and the horizon in every direction. I've never seen a sky like that.

Before we knew it, it was evening and we were tired again. Kebby left us at the house of a woman named Martha and said that our host, Brian, would come for us soon.

We went to a shop and bought four packages of spaghetti and tomato sauce and returned to Martha. She gave me a metal bucket and put coals in it. Then, she lit them and positioned me in front of the house. She showed me how to swing the bucket back and forth, feeding the fire. Once it was hot, we boiled water over the coals and cooked the spaghetti.

There was a plank of wood out front with a checkerboard painted on in white, along with a warning: "DO NOT CHEAT IN ORDER

TO WIN." The pieces were beer bottle tops. I sat next to the board on a short tree stump but didn't play.

We must have been a spectacle, all haggard and in matching t-shirts with the logo of Uncle Ben's Instant Rice, official sponsor of the US team at the 1996 Atlanta Olympics, emblazoned across the front. George pulled them out of the garage and gave them to us when we left Albania, saying we looked like messes and needed new clothes.

After dinner, Brian came and took us to his house on the dusty outskirts of Lusaka.

Brian and his wife Dora helped us inside. Both of them are tall and kind. Dora just had a baby last week. His name is Andrew, after the team leader of the World Race team that was here in April.

"Really?" we asked. "You named your baby after a Racer?" We thought it was a joke.

"Yes, he asked me to, so I said I would," she said.

We were exhausted, but we stayed up to talk and watch TV and mention that we hadn't eaten nshima yet. And so, at 10:30, Brian and Dora prepared us a *second* dinner with nshima, watermelon, and chicken. We were forbidden from doing dishes. They told us to go to bed and sleep in tomorrow.

They flush toilet paper here, but I threw it on the ground by accident. I assumed there would be a bin there.

Everyone is happy, smart, snappy. I'm in a big room with fresh paint and its own bath. Courtney and Heidi share a queen bed and I'm on my sleeping pad.

June 2
Lusaka, Zambia

Lusaka is a big city but its roads are unpaved. There is a big, new football stadium that would be white and gleaming were it not covered in red dust. Near the stadium is Brian's church and our ministry base, Great in Christ Pentecostal Church.

The church is made of cinder blocks and has a corrugated tin roof that lets the wind in. The floor is red dirt that gets everywhere, so before services, they sweep the white plastic chairs clean. There's a stage with sofas in slipcovers (red dirt in the seams) and a glass coffee table. There's a sound system. There's a digital clock mounted on the walls.

It feels light and friendly inside. I'm happy to be here for the month.

Down the road from the church is a tin shack where we can buy Cokes. There's a mall somewhere nearby too, where we can go for WiFi and groceries.

June 3
Lusaka, Zambia

This month is all about evangelizing and I'm dreading it.

Evangelize. That word just means telling people the gospel, which means good news. What's the good news? The good news is about God creating us, loving us, and living in us. It's about God coming to us, identifying as one of us in a human called Jesus, suffering and living and dying in our world. It's about Jesus unbreaking our brokenness by becoming broken himself. It is about the Spirit of God, the Breath of God, Who's always with us, letting humanity comprehend God and life and people and reality more and more... that's good news. That's mysterious. That's what I believe. That's my foundation.

But *evangelism*? Yuck. That word is fraught with negative stereotypes. And I've seen them, all those tricks that employ efficiency to save souls as fast as possible—all at the cost of relationships. I've seen the threatening questions and cold calls and ugly brochures and snide logic meant to trap people into admitting they believe in a higher power. All of the tactics I've learned to spread the gospel makes the truth ring so hollow that I start doubting it myself.

Committing to relationships is true. Letting friends witness my faith as I live life is true. But when it's about going up to strangers and telling them they have to believe in Jesus right now or burn in hell, and to please repeat a prayer after me so I can move on to the next person… when it's about tallying saved souls, or dismissing the narratives of others by saying the Bible trumps their own honest interpretations of this painful, beautiful world… it weirds me out and pisses me off and I don't want any part of it. It's *bad*. It's *fucked up*.

I know this because I've been there. I evangelized so much in college and it didn't even work.

I sat at tables with candies by the bookstore. I'd say, "Wanna Life Saver? Suck on that and I'll tell you about the *ultimate* Life Saver." I came back from conferences fired up about God and shared the gospel with my roommates and it was never not weird. I put my faith on view over and over, and I was met with warm indifference and tactful hostility. It was embarrassing and disheartening but I kept at it, until the things I was learning in my world religion classes began eclipsing the things I was preaching, and I grew doubtful and angry about God not showing up more. I started fearing that God was fake, or wimpy, or perhaps altogether different than what I'd been thinking.

Now, I have a *degree* in acknowledging the world's wealth of religious traditions. And how am I using that degree? By making the incomprehensible choice to become a missionary and espouse the primacy of one.

But bouncing around my brain, it's still there, that slew of academic, pluralistic, liberal, subversive, problematizing, marginalized, marginalizing voices. Of *course*, I do not know what to make of Jesus being the only way to God. I do not know if the way I was taught to interpret the Bible is *the* way, or how to view Judaism or the Hebrew Bible, or how God is in the world, or heaven and hell, or how miraculous healings work, or if the resurrection of Jesus was literal, or if there's a God at all. Who *wouldn't* doubt that now and then?

It's hard to say I doubt all this stuff to the Christian world, because if I don't have faith, my pastor will want to take me to a quiet Starbucks and buy me a caramel macchiato and pray the doubts away. But I must say all this stuff because I can't be the only one who struggles with all that goes into being a Christian. It's hard. It's weird. The Church is too quick to shame the people who can't accept the weird stuff. But when I think about it, it's all weird stuff.

I know deep down, past my education and personal struggles, that evangelism isn't about having it all sorted out, but about letting God's strength be perfect in my weakness and being present with other people. I know that God's working in ways I can't see and I don't have to worry about anything.

And yes, fine, I admit that the kind of evangelism we do on the Race is often lovely. My squad is fantastic at encountering people with open eyes and flexible hearts. We let Jesus speak through us and trust that God's guiding everyone on their own journey... but even as I say that, I wonder if it is possible that I'm just making excuses to abrogate responsibility for my words and undercut the disruptive power of our presence as foreign missionaries.

I hope God can use me, hang ups and all. *Something* big and real captivated me and brought me here. *Something* overshadowed a typical post-college trajectory and made my heart yearn to get vaccinated, shovel pig shit, pick out lice, and preach the coming of a Kingdom I don't understand in the company of 40 random people. Maybe it was just a lust for adventure, but even if it was, who cares, I'm here now, and something is making my heart burn enough to stay in the game. So, I'm going to experience this reluctance and go door to door anyway, taking the steps assigned, waiting to see what great splendor prompted them.

But I still don't want to.

June 5
Lusaka, Zambia

Team Oak is making our own breakfasts and lunches this month. With our food budget, that will mean peanut butter and jelly sandwiches on the cheapest bread available (usually there are bits of straw baked into it) and potato chips. Dora and Brian will cook us

115

dinner. They will make us a lot of nshima, greens, and *kapenta*, a type of tiny sardine that comes dried and crispy.

Okay, no, you know what my real issue with evangelism is?

It is exhausting.

I can't stand being forced to go house to house, meeting people, chatting with them, praying for them, and weeping with them, only to do it all over again next door. I'm always wiped out. I never want to read my Bible at the end of the day. I just want to read a big fat fantasy novel and eat junk food.

Maybe I'm not an atheist asshole. Maybe I'm just an introvert.

June 6
Lusaka, Zambia

Growing up Christian, I'd often hear from people who had just returned from mission trips. They'd be in movies, or on the radio, or at church. The most impressive ones had been in Africa. Never a specific country, just Africa. They'd put up slideshows at the 9:30 service and talk about how even though they'd gone to serve the locals, the locals had really served *them*.

The slideshows would have photos of them with smiling locals, them eating barbecued snakes, them holding dripping paint brushes in front of badly-painted houses. I couldn't tell why the missionaries had helped people in those countries, but it looked like they had fun and came home with a tan, and they were very popular at the post-service coffee hour.

So, from seeing people like that, and from hearing of stereotypes of Americans abroad in books and movies, I have in mind this problematic caricature of the consummate missionary, this Christian of the highest order. She drills a well with one hand, passes out freshly translated Bibles with the other, smiles down at the grateful orphans clinging to her hips, all while rattling off a loud, long, impromptu sermon on her "called-not-qualified" tongue.

I know from my education and common sense that this image is rooted in a tradition of people with light skin going to people with dark skin and telling them to adopt the former's culture. It is an outdated image, an image that has been used to undermine, rather than defend, the legitimacy of the majority of the world. But nevertheless, in this country more than the previous five, I feel such pressure to be that caricature.

I feel the pressure from the people here and the people who donated money for me to be here. And I chose to go on this trip, so I am, to some extent, choosing to embody that stereotype. Say what you want about my motives, but I am a rich white girl with a college degree from the States, and I am in Zambia, and I am here to serve. For those facts alone, the people who sent me here and the people who have hosted me here think I'm hot shit.

All this was obvious today. We took a day off from evangelism and took on a chaotic whirlwind of ministry.

In the morning, we walked a half mile down the road to an orphanage to play games with the kids at recess. There was a trampoline made of old tires on the playground and I jumped on it one time and it broke. The kids laughed at me and tattled on me to the lady who ran the orphanage. Then, the girls braided my hair so tight I thought my scalp was ripping.

After the orphanage, Brian drove us to a house church in a neighborhood of Lusaka. We met a man named Prophet Paul, who had a big belly and barely spoke English. He walked us into a little dark house.

It was warm in the front room. The sofas were upholstered with fleece. A white cabinet full of dishes stood inexplicably in the center. A poster of a preacher and a calendar with his face on it hung on the wall.

And the house was full of women. They were singing loud songs in Bemba, Nyanja, and English, and clapping complex, precise rhythms. They were dancing in a circle and taking turns in the middle. They were wearing long colorful fabric wraps called *chitenges* around their waists and wearing babies on their backs. One chubby baby was nearly asleep on his mom's shoulder, a half-eaten chicken foot in his hand.

I didn't know how we could ever match their energy, but when it was time, Heidi stood and shared her testimony. Arden preached about God transforming us. We kept dipping back into songs until all of a sudden, we were pouring out of the house and stampeding through the neighborhood. Someone said we were going to "an elderly man." We saw him sitting in a chair. Brian said he couldn't sit up straight or walk at all, until two years ago when people prayed for him. Then he was fine for a while, but two months ago he started getting weak, so now we had to pray again. People think he will die soon. We all sang and prayed, this horde of women.

I was caught up in watching all this unfold more than I was participating, when I saw that Prophet Paul was pointing at me.

"Pray for us."

Arden said later it looked like I'd been planning to say something. I hadn't been. But I prayed, for the old man under the tree in the chair, born in 1940, named Abel, abandoned by his kids, with family far away in Livingstone, to walk and be restored.

Jason told Abel to look at the crowd around him. "Look at how many people love you," he said.

Heidi told him to stand up and move, and everyone must have thought she was going to do some big thing because they crowded in. But she wanted to study his legs because she works with the elderly in a physical therapy clinic. Abel stood and walked in a tiny circle. I don't know if he could beforehand or not, but it took a long time to seat him again. Once he was sitting, Heidi prescribed him some exercises.

Then we sang more and went back to the house church where a feast was waiting for us. Nshima, chicken, chicken, chicken, steamed okra, sweet potatoes in peanut sauce, veggie this, veggie that, I don't know. Orange juice, the kind that comes concentrated for you to dilute with water you sure hope has been filtered. Our team was told to eat. When we asked who made the food, six women came out from the back and knelt on the floor before us and we clapped for them. But they just clapped for us.

Then, we prayed for them. They wanted us to pray for them to find good husbands and have enough money.

There were children milling about at the door, so we prayed for them, too. As we exited the house and piled back into Brian's car, dozens and dozens more children appeared in the street. We drove out of the village and this flash flood of kids followed us, running and waving, smacking the back window of the car and climbing on the bumper whenever we stopped.

It was an amazing day. It was fun to not know what was going on, to be ushered from house to house and song to song.

But who are we, that women should kneel before us, that pastors should demand prayers and messages from us?

When we came home, there was a new mattress in our room for me. I knew that it was pointless to refuse it, to insist that I was happy to sleep on the floor, that the comforter he had laid over my sleeping pad was already a luxury. It was humbling and like every other over-the-top act of honor today, I just accepted it.

For dinner, we had sweet potatoes and hot chocolate. Arden and I went with Dora and Brian to their friend Pastor Drake's house because he has a gadget that will let us play movies from American flash drives on African TVs.

Then, our team and Brian and Dora's family decided to have a movie night. We turned on *Brave*. As I watched the movie, I felt like I was just with my family, but then I looked around and saw they were black and white and we were in a house on the other side of the world. At the climax of the movie, the power went out. We laughed and went to bed.

Before sleeping, I stepped outside and looked up. The sky was bright with the moon and city lights.

All the what-business-do-I-have-here stuff is bouncing around in my head, but at the same time, I just love being here. I love it. I'm happy it hasn't even been a week. Every day I wake up worried about evangelism or preaching, and every day, I'm bowled over by how cool this place is.

June 7
Lusaka, Zambia

We went to a baby shower at Great in Christ Church. It was supposed to start at 2:00 but we knew not to believe that. We arrived before 2:00 and sat in white plastic chairs in the open air, cinder block sanctuary. Music was thumping and green and orange streamers hung from the rafters. New strollers and bassinets sat in rows on the stage.

It started at 3:30. I don't know who the shower was for, but the matron (the mother of the mother-to-be) was wearing nothing but white and dancing all over the place. It was mostly women again. There were presents and sermons and dancing and singing and food.

Michael, a young teen, sat next to me and explained things. At one point he told me to raise my hand, so I did. People raise their hands a lot, usually because a preacher says, "Raise your hand if you love the Lord!"

The women with their hands raised went to the front.

"Michael, why am I raising my hand?" I asked.

"You're not pregnant," he said. "They're praying for people who aren't mothers yet, that you have many babies."

I put my hand down. I watched all the ladies up front get slain by the Spirit.

A woman saw my hair clip—a beautiful blue and yellow beaded barrette I bought in Antigua—and said, "I like your hair piece. Give it to me."

I wasn't sure if in this culture, people are supposed to fork things over when asked, so I sadly removed it from my hair and gave it to her and she started laughing and her friend cracked up, too.

Later I asked Dora if it's customary to give people your stuff when they ask for it and she said, "Uh, no."

June 8
Lusaka, Zambia

Today I preached about how God provides for and surprises us. At the end of my sermon I read Ephesians 3:20.

"'Now to him,'" I proclaimed, "'who is able to do far more abundantly than all that we ask or think, according to the power at work within us, to Him be the glory in the Church and in Christ Jesus throughout all generations, forever and ever. Amen.' And, um, yeah!"

I went to my seat. Arden said I had a gift for teaching and that made me feel good.

Pastor Brian started preaching some more about "the abundance of God," and then he invited people up who wanted prayer for God to provide abundantly for them. They lined up at the foot of the stage and Brian went left to right, laying hands on their heads. One lady fell down as soon as he touched her, slain in the Spirit.

Someone told us to go up and minister, too.

"Do we have to knock them over?" I asked Courtney out of the corner of my mouth as we went to the stage. She shrugged. I found a woman in a white shirt and put my arm around her and started praying for her. I didn't know what to say and I felt this pressure to perform somehow, to be yelling and rocking, to fit in and not look like the poser I was. Funny how we have to be loud here to blend in.

I prayed for the lady in white and then stood there for a minute with my hand on her. She said something, but the music was so loud I don't know what it was. I put my ear next to her mouth, expecting something tearful or grateful, or maybe if I could please slay her now. But she said:

"Can I go?"

"Oh, sorry. Yes, all done!"

June 9
Lusaka, Zambia

Zambia is not as grueling as I expected. It's also more fulfilling than I expected.

I love living with Oak. Being alone as a team is so much sweeter than dividing time with everyone on the squad. More than anything in the world right now, more than any place or ministry right now, it is sweet to be in the same room as these five other people. Each thing that goes wrong, every hard piece of feedback given, every tired day of ministry... we are falling into an effortless rhythm of living together through it.

It is morning now and we are hopefully going to eat eggs with all the red peppers that are stinking up the broken fridge. The peppers have been in there for a week and all our food tastes like them, especially the peanut butter. The peanut butter doesn't need to be in there, but if we leave it out, Brian's kids will find it and eat it all.

June 11
Lusaka, Zambia

We joined the church for an outreach at a market. There were about 50 kids there and instead of paying attention to the service, I made pictures in the dirt with a stick and they crowded me, guessing what I was drawing.

Heidi took a photo of me without my knowledge. She showed it to me and I was surprised: I look like a missionary. The transformation is complete. I'm wearing a bright blue blouse and a brown chitenge around my waist. My hair is red and dusty and braided, and I stand, regal and benevolent, in a crowd of Zambian children. I don't look like a skeptic ignoring a sermon. I look like someone who always believes in Jesus, who wants to be wanted by the poor and downtrodden, who gets ten minutes to present at the 9:30 service.

June 15
Lusaka, Zambia

We went to Pastor Drake's church today. It was horrific.

Drake said everything that morning was of God and for God and from God, but *beating* demons out of people? Letting the pastor and the North Americans sit on the couch in the front drinking juice while everyone else sat in plastic chairs? The eternity of music and dancing and strange preaching and exorcism after exorcism?

The service lasted three hours.

First came the music. Pastor Drake bullied us for not dancing and singing hard enough. He called us out from the pulpit: "You *muzungus*, you white kids, you are standing there like cyborgs! You are not dancing with joy for the Lord!"

They made me dance in front of everyone. A tall woman pulled me up and tied a *chitenge* around my hips. I thought the yard of colorful fabric was for modesty, even though I was already wearing a long skirt, but she tied it tight around my ass and said, "Now it's easier for us to see you shake it!"

I smiled, I laughed, and I tried really hard to find the good in it and imitate the movements of the other people up there, but it felt so wrong. People whooped and yelled and cheered, but I wanted it to be over and returned to my seat as soon as there was a break in the music. My legs are now weak from swaying for three hours. Swaying was enough movement to escape being taunted by the pastor, but not enough to bodily condone what was going on.

Next came the preaching. Pastor Drake gave this bullshit sermon about being joyful all the time.

"The joy of the Lord is your strength," he said, "so if you are not joyful you are weak. You must be happy always."

Then came the deliverances, and that was the worst part. A woman came to the center of the room for prayer because she couldn't find work. She vomited into a grocery bag as Drake stood over her and screamed at the demon of "employers not being able to see her credentials." He kept pushing her around on the floor. She continued to throw up into her plastic bag while everyone around her screamed and praised God, because this was supposed to be the demon coming out.

I wanted to put my hand on that woman's head as people slapped and screamed at the demon in her. But I stood at a distance and prayed, *Peace, peace, peace on you, is this normal, is this okay, will you be okay, I don't know what to do…*

I know that this is not my culture. I realize that maybe this kind of church service is normal. But the pressure, confrontation, and violence I saw today… I didn't and couldn't see God in it. In fact, I refused to see God in it. That service emptied me in the worst way. I couldn't connect to it. I cannot digest it.

The chintz and yelling and demon-slaying… it would never convert me.

June 20
Lusaka, Zambia

I'm all prayed out. We go to all these church services and they tell us to pray for things like the exchange rates between the Zambian kwacha and the American dollar. I'm always faking it and it is tiring. I don't want to read the Bible anymore in my spare time, because we spend our ministry hours preaching about how it promises health and riches, even though it doesn't.

June 21
Lusaka, Zambia

Oak went to Chilanga to see a church there and some lions in cages. But I was home sick and homesick. The electricity was off for the day, so it was very dark, and I was alone under the net with my laptop. I was scared I was coming down with something… something bad. I was so relieved when Oak returned and Brian turned on the generator.

June 23
Lusaka, Zambia

Something is wrong with my body. My appetite is gone. I only eat when my stomach can't take the emptiness, and then I eat just enough to dull the pain.

We leave Lusaka in two days and it's bittersweet. I need the debrief and I'm excited to go to Livingstone and see Victoria Falls. But this month has been monumental and I am sad to leave these people.

Sandra is no longer in our room because she went to stay with another family. I think she might have stolen my hand mirror. I don't really care, but now I have no way to look at myself. There are no mirrors in the house and my iPhone's always filthy.

I've felt annoyed at my team lately, but I think that's because I haven't been feeling well. I am run down.

They said it'd be hard. They said there'd be big bugs. They said we'd get sick. And I am sick, but still, this was the month I met Africa at golden hour from the bed of a pickup truck.

The month I saw my first baobab tree and the month of dumbfounding hospitality.

The month I preached sermons, sometimes with a few minutes to prepare.

The month of different stars.

The month we were invited into dozens and dozens of strangers' houses to eat or drink tea.

The month we were asked daily, "Have you eaten nshima?"

The month we answered daily, "Yes, we've eaten nshima."

The month our host family bought us new mattresses so we wouldn't have to keep sleeping on the floor.

The month I learned to like peanut butter and jelly sandwiches.

The month of winter in June.

The month of not calling home a single time.

The month we were stared at everywhere we went and evangelism and church dancing and roaches and earwigs.

The month I heard Katy Perry's new song "Dark Horse" and then four hours of Christmas music in a coffee shop.

The month my hair doubled in volume from dust.

The month of being given my very own chitenge to use as a skirt or towel or scarf.

The month of cleaning a hospital, of 72 languages, of blessings from strangers, of seeing God work in differences, of hard conversations of what it means to be a disciple.

The month of a thousand handshakes, a thousand curtsies.

The month least like home.

The month of homesickness.

The month of being at home anyway.

June 24
Lusaka, Zambia

They don't tell you about the 10 Percent Club when you sign up for the Race. To be in this club, you have to be one of the elite few Racers who goes the whole year without pooping their pants.

I knew I was out of the 10 Percent Club this morning when I woke up and decided to fart. Instead of a puff of relief, I felt something warm and moist and I leapt out of bed to save my clean sleeping bag liner.

Should I see a doctor? I guess it'll have to be in Livingstone at the debrief. Today's the last day in Lusaka.

June 25
Livingstone, Zambia

Being here blesses me and consoles me. I'm sleeping in my tent at Jollyboys Backpackers, with some space and privacy. The squad is back together and it's great.

There are rooms here, but we're staying in a grassy yard in our tents to save money. I like staying in my tent. It's warm and orange and solitary. I'm tired. I needed this break, but I wasn't desperate or panicky for it like earlier in the year. I'm not too homesick. I'm stronger.

June 26
Livingstone, Zambia
Fully funded today. People have now given me $15,500 to take this journey.

I am currently taking expired ciprofloxacin I found in a free pile at the hostel. Feeling hunger pains but no hunger.

Jayce and I bought chicken and veggies, and were going to cook dinner together, but I started feeling so awful that I had to go sit in my tent.

I grew more terrified that something was seriously wrong by the second. I was dizzy and foggy and lethargic. Panic took over me before I knew what was going on. I was chugging water to stave off dehydration, but it was too late, I was passing out, the needles were coming, the fear, the dehydration, the IV, the flight home, my weakness, my failure, malaria, parasites, panic, cancer, danger, game over, game over...

I stumbled out of my tent and the first two people I saw were Heidi and Mateo. I said I needed help and they took me in a taxi to the hospital just down the street. I felt so terrible that I was fully resigned to IVs and blood tests, but all they did was take my blood pressure. Normal. Temperature. Normal. I steeled myself ready for the malaria test, but the doctor just came in, felt my stomach, and prescribed me new ciprofloxacin.

Now, C Squad is in an empty church, worshipping again to the same songs we've been singing all year, and I'm famished. I don't know if it's food I need or Jesus.

So, I'm opening to the sixth chapter of the Gospel of John, the part about Jesus saying He's the Bread of Life, and I'm reading. I'm not reading the Bible like I normally read the Bible— I'm not savoring each word and chewing the phrases over. I'm reading it like a starving man, in gasps and gulps, not caring what it tastes like, just knowing I need the calories.

I've been ignoring the Bible in my private life lately because it has been my job all month to preach it. Now I'm realizing how hungry I've been for it.

June 27
Livingstone, Zambia

Jacob says that if you eat a whole clove of garlic a day, mosquitos won't bite you and you'll never have heart disease. Every day, he minces a garlic clove with his Leatherman and offers it to people. I like to knock it back with water in the open-air kitchen here at the hostel. It makes me feel like a badass.

Staying at the hostels in between ministries is one of the keenest pleasures of the Race. There are no papers to write, no buildings to paint, no sermons to preach. I can sit in a hammock all day and talk with whomever I please about anything. Maybe that's what it is to be old. Maybe that's what park benches are for.

And my team, Oak. We have this gorgeous ability to split anything between the six of us: chocolate bars, single cookies, half bottles of flat Pepsi. We share everything and the grace we have for each other in the small things is the greatest indicator of the sense of ease we have in each other's company and in our happy, albeit temporary, lack of property.

The Race is now over halfway over. I know I have changed. My hair is red. Sometimes I wake up in the morning and I don't remember what country I'm in. When I use public toilets, I don't avoid the ones that haven't been flushed. I eat peanut butter even though

I don't like it. I'm not scared of lice or of being put on the spot to give a sermon.

I bet most of the changes are changes I don't even see. But if I went home today, I'd have one thing to tell people considering The Race:

Don't worry.

Just don't.

About anything.

Don't worry about packing because you'll have what you need, buy what you want, and dump the rest. Don't worry about food because everyone eats and that doesn't change out here. Don't worry about preaching because you always have something to say. Don't worry about fundraising. Don't worry about squatty potties. Don't worry about travel days. Don't worry about gaining weight or losing muscle. Don't worry when there's conflict on your team. Don't worry when you're not hearing God speak. Don't worry when you're bad at your job. Don't worry when the charter bus with all your gear has disappeared at 2 a.m. and you're alone in the night in Albania. Don't worry when the border people want to unpack your things for inspection. Don't worry about ATM fees. Don't worry when you hear weird doctrines. Don't worry when you get lice. Don't worry about mismatched clothes. Don't worry about malaria. Don't worry about how spiritual you are or aren't. Don't worry about team changes. Don't worry if you're making a big enough difference. Don't worry about door to door evangelism.

Life's circumstances nearly always require action but they never require anxiety.

USA: eating rice at training camp days after meeting each other (Nicole Bouza)

USA: a typical scene: World Races sleeping on airport floors (Nicole Bouza)

Honduras: my team's bedroom during the first month of the Race

Honduras: Brazen Hearts eating junk food, as usual

Guatemala: getting into scsrubs
before a day of work in a hospital
sterilization room (Nicole Bouza)

Guatemala:
visiting Iglesia
de La Merced
in Antigua

Guatemala: our task one day was simply to make this rock go away. We couldn't. (Nicole Bouza)

Guatemala: the 41 tents of C Squad

El Salvador:
playing mandolin
for my team
Brazen "Butts"
(Nicole Bouza)

Bulgaria: messing
around in Sofia
(Nicole Bouza)

Albania: Tucker,
the puppy we
rescued from
the dumpster

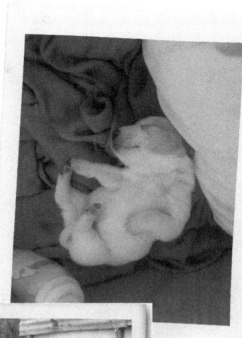

Albania: Knee
deep in pig poop
(Nicole Bouza)

Albania: C Squad sitting on a mountain of chicken poop at the end of a long day (Nicole Bouza)

Zambia: in a church member's house during door-to-door evangelism (Jayce Van Der Linden)

Zambia: painting a new sign for Great in Christ Church, our ministry home for June (Courtney Radley)

Zambia: Sugarcane became a staple in our diet.

Zambia: watching the sun set over Victoria Falls (Nicole Bouza)

Malawi: a broken-down bus: just one of many travel setbacks. (Jayce Van Der Linden)

Malawi: another broken-down bus! (Jayce Van Der Linden)

Malawi: preaching a sermon with a translator

139

Malawi: C Squad's packs piled high in a corridor after our first attempt to enter Mozambique failed

Mozambique: building a ping pong table at the boys' home (Jayce Van Der Linden)

Mozambique: our ministry site and home for August. Spot the teammate in the mango tree

Mozambique:
C Squad piling into a truck bed

Mozambique: crossing a 3.5-kilometer bridge on foot during our 55-hour exit from Mozambique

Thailand: playing music and offering free prayer at the night market in Chiang Mai

Thailand: my parents and I touring a town outside of the city.

Cambodia: waiting for tuk tuks late at night in Phnom Penh

Cambodia: playing soccer with our seminary friends

Cambodia: my belongings took a beating on the World Race.

Cambodia: I taught English, geography, religion, and writing for a month. And the word "mafia."

Malaysia: visiting a house church

145

USA: C Squad (Nicole Bouza)

COUNTRY 7:
MALAWI

In which I lose trust in public
transportation, grieve a death,
and eat sugarcane in the
back of a truck.

July 1
Mabuya Camp in Lilongwe, Malawi

It is 7:20 in the morning and we are in Lilongwe, Malawi's capital.

Nearly 24 hours ago, we left Livingstone, Zambia on a bus proudly touted as "only three weeks old." That just meant that there was still plastic on half the seats and the air conditioning wasn't hooked up yet.

King Kong was playing on the overhead screens when we boarded. The new version, with Jack Black and Adrian Brody and Naomi Watts.

I actually watched *King Kong* recently, in Bulgaria. I didn't like the action sequences because they diluted the already-thin plot. But I liked it more this time because of the subtitles, or, should I say, "sub-iles," because they lacked the letter T. The characters said things like, "Ge on he boa, before i's oo lae," and, at tense moments, "Chris!"

Once the bus was on its way, the movie started from the beginning and we watched it again. So, on the World Race, I have now seen the Jack Black version of *King Kong* two and a half times.

After *King Kong* we watched *Monkey Trouble*. *Monkey Trouble* is a nineties flick about Eva, a girl who doesn't know what to bring for show and tell and doesn't like her baby brother Jack. She meets a monkey named Dodger and gets caught in a web of lies trying to hide Dodger from her parents. Dodger is trained to steal, but Eva teaches him to stop shoplifting and take her mom's jewelry, instead. Eventually Baby Jack says his first word: "monkeys." Eva's family finally understands everything and they take down the bad guys. Then Eva takes both Jack and Dodger to show and tell.

After the monkey movies, I spent a long time sleeping in the center aisle, eating snacks, and learning how to take care of my new dreadlock, which Kelsey made with a lice comb under the light of a headlamp.

At 10:00 p.m. we stopped in a dim, bustling marketplace. We found a public restroom across the street. It was a smelly squatty potty with two-inch cockroaches scuttling on the pockmarked doorway. They were gross, but we were brave like Adrian Brody when he fights the giant bugs in *King Kong* in order to save Naomi Watts, and we entered the stalls and pulled down our pants to hover over the dark abysses.

We came to the Malawi border at 3:00 a.m., and all of us staggered off the bus into the cold, winter night. We waited in line to get our Zambia exit stamps, then wandered under a million stars into Malawi.

I used to fear long bus rides. I would find out how long they were supposed to take, and I'd keep track of the time and worry if I didn't get enough sleep.

But now, I know that the bus rides will be longer than expected, we will all be tired… and everything will be okay.

Oak still has 356 kilometers more to go to reach Mzuzu, our month's destination. But for now, C Squad is at a hostel in Lilongwe, where we will spend a day and a night to rest.

I took a weird, deep nap and woke up when it was hot in my tent. I stripped off my socks and two sweaters and went to the bathroom and felt drugged. Arden and I sat on the grass outside his tent, dipping what food we had left from the travel day in Nutella. Jayce and Daniel showed up, and we played Monopoly Deal and drank instant coffee.

It was spectacular.

At Christian conferences at Vassar (my university), I would go read my Bible and worship for hours a day. I'd wear myself out praying until the last night, when I'd finally have magnificent, emotional, tearful breakthroughs about God's love, or trustworthiness, or power.

Those breakthroughs were great moments. They changed me for the better. I wouldn't be here if I hadn't had such dramatic experiences of God. But, even though I knew better, part of me thought that the World Race would be like that: 11 months of being spiritually high. That's what the videos and wise, tanned, tattooed aesthetic of its alumni suggest.

But it is not like that. Human temperaments are multifaceted. After a long day of ministry, I need a novel and, if it won't "cause the local believers to stumble," a beer. After praying all day, I don't need to pray more. I need to stay up late making "that's what she said" jokes with my team. This trip isn't a sprint or a radical retreat from the world into the Kingdom. It's a different lifestyle. I haven't become a caricature of a missionary because I'm on a mission trip.

And when I let myself love every little luxury and annoyance of this trip, not just the "Christian" parts, that's when I love it most.

I love this life. I love it. I love it and I don't want another one. I love the oscillations of discomfort and ease. I love the changing landscapes. I love the food. I love how much I laugh. I love how instant coffee is a religious experience. I love my dreadlock. And most of all, I love the people I'm with. I love sitting on the grass and dipping things in Nutella with my friends.

July 2
Mzuzu, Malawi
It's night. We're staying at Mzuzu Pentecostal Church. We sleep in the attics above the sanctuary.

July 4
Mzuzu, Malawi
I like our hosts Moses and Susan. Moses spent time at a seminary in Texas and he has a photo on the wall of himself with a bunch of big smiling white guys at a rodeo. He has a deep, kind laugh.

Susan is kind and quiet, too. She loves to cook and when she's done cooking, she sits on the couch or on a chair with her feet up and the brazier nearby. It's cold here.

"Have you had nsima?" she asked when we arrived.

"Nshima?"

"Here, we say *nsima*."

We walk from the church to their house in the morning for breakfast, which is primarily white bread, fake butter, cane sugar, oatmeal, and Nescafe. We eat all this good stuff and watch TV. It's like being a kid again, with a mom cooking for us and letting us watch cartoons and the fact that everything except the coffee is white.

Ministry is the same as last month: evangelism. We're effectively joining the youth group and doing all their activities. The youth group is mostly twenty-somethings, though. It's nice. We are the same age, at least, and that's enough common ground to build friendships. They take us out evangelizing and translate for us.

Like last month, the official language of this country is English, but there are actually many. Nyanja is here a bit, but most people speak Chichewa.

It's a mile walk to Mzuzu Coffee Den where we can get WiFi.

July 5
Mzuzu, Malawi

Our host Pastor Moses asked if we'd ever eaten rat. We all said no.

"It's nice," he said.

People here don't say food is good. They say it's *nice*.

And they don't say, "I'll pick you up later." They say, "I'll pick you later."

And you don't eat lunch. You *take* lunch.

July 8
Mzuzu, Malawi

We put a sheet of butcher paper on the wall; on it, the team is putting their prayer requests.

The suffering is overwhelming! Grudges, sick loved ones, poverty. How can I open myself up to that? Is that what it means to really pray? Is prayer hard work because it means choosing to feel an ounce of someone's endless pain? In choosing to be overwhelmed by evil, can I hope to overwhelm it someday?

That's what Jesus did. Jesus opened himself to the yuck. He let it scare, hurt, and kill Him.

But I do not want to put the time in to suffer right now. I have *New Girl* reruns on my computer and I basically pray professionally, so I'd rather watch TV in my downtime. Plus, I don't want a God that comes alongside me in my sufferings. I want a God that makes everything good always. Can God's presence in people's lives really redeem the horror and chaos of this world?

Funny that I'm asking these questions. I've been a Christian my entire life and I still don't know how it works.

July 11
Mzuzu, Malawi

We were helping out at a school and a girl named Vanessa asked me, "Tell me the truth, is there really a God?"

Well shit, Vanessa, I sure hope so, I thought.

I do believe in God, but I'm scared I don't believe enough. I'm scared I'll drift, or that someone or something will convince me otherwise. I'm a Christian now, but will I be one in 25 years? When will it get hard? What if what I hope and believe turns out to be different from what is true, and I have to leave the hope for the real truth? What if I stop believing and don't have the guts to tell people? I've been a Christian my whole life. I know how to do it. I could fake it. I already fake it sometimes. What if I'm already kidding myself and there's no God but I just keep lying to save face—

"Yes, Vanessa, there is a God. But it's good to ask questions."

July 14
Mzuzu, Malawi

Prince Edward came to get us for evangelizing today and he was carrying a slim New Testament in one hand and a complete, heavy Bible with ribbon bookmarks and maps and concordances in the other.

"This," he said, waving the New Testament, "is a pistol." He tossed it onto the pew.

"But *this*," he declared, holding the Bible aloft, "is a machine gun. Now, let's go to battle."

July 16
Mzuzu, Malawi

Our shower this month is cold and terrifying. The concrete building it's in hosts what we've begun calling The Helicopter. It's some sort of incredible wasp we've only seen a few times. Mostly it buzzes up in the rafters. It's huge, the size of a child's fist, and it sounds like a lawnmower.

July 17
Mzuzu, Malawi

Jayce and I sat in a church pew and had a great conversation. He gave me feedback: keep pursuing, he said. Like, keep going after my passions and keep engaging and thinking.

Sometimes I'm afraid I'm annoying the team when I rant about my evangelism issues or doubts, but he said not to stop and that it's good my brain works the way it does.

We were doing more door to door evangelism, and a path led us to a small, sharp hillside with a dried-up garden and a small house with green grass around it. We walked down to the door. The owner wasn't there, but his mother, Christina, was. Christina was breaking up dirt to plant sweet potatoes. With church member Anna translating, Arden and I explained that we were with Mzuzu Pentecostal Church, and we were missionaries from America, and we were in the neighborhood to encourage and pray with people and help them in any ways they needed. We asked if there were any areas in her life that she needed encouragement, or if she had any prayer requests. Same stuff we say every time.

Christina hesitated, then touched her eyes and said she had a hard time seeing, as well as a bad cough and body pains. So, Christina, Arden, Annalise, and I sat on our butts in the red dirt, as usual. I opened my Bible and aimlessly thumbed through it, not sure what to say. This is what we do when we go door to door: we talk to people, and then are expected to encourage them by talking about a Bible verse or some story that can pertain to their lives. We missionaries who have come from so far away are always supposed to know what to say. But we don't. At least, I don't. I never do, but I pretend.

I have been playing the part of a messenger from God with a word at dozens and dozens of houses this year. Even though I'm supposed to be listening to what God might be telling us to say, I've been doing this so long that I'm numb. I literally thumb through my Bible until I land on a passage that I can say a smart thing about. The people I'm talking to think I'm giving them "a word," but it's like I'm making up a horoscope. I'm pulling impressive words out of my butt and leaning on the rhetoric of my indoctrination. My heart is not in it. I'm faking it.

But I ought to be telling myself that in 2 Corinthians 6:8-10, Paul writes:

> "We are treated as impostors, and yet are true; as unknown, and yet well known; as dying, and behold, we live; as punished, and yet not killed; as sorrowful, yet always rejoicing; as poor, yet making many rich; as having nothing, yet possessing everything."

I can identify with some of those dichotomies. I treat myself like a fake missionary. I feel poor when I go out, like I don't have enough words or love for myself, let alone stranger after stranger.

Yet when I meet people, whether it's nerves or a pinch of adrenaline or good manners or the Holy Spirit, I find myself smiling and using energy I didn't know I had. Somehow, against all my reason, the work we're doing is true.

I know that because at nearly every house, we are thanked and called blessings and commended for working hard for God. And our forced, feeble mumblings of encouragement are actually precious words from God that make many feel rich.

I still didn't know what to say to Christina. I had landed on the eighth chapter of John, where Jesus calls Himself the Light of the World. I said something about that. My words prompted some thoughts from Arden, and after both of us had shared, Christina told us something more.

She had 12 children but only one was still alive: the son whose house we were sitting in front of. He was troubled, she told us. He would disappear and not say where he was off to. He was trying to finish school, but it was very hard for him. She was sad and out of energy. She said she was staying alive for him, but every day was a struggle.

What do you say to that?

Arden, Annalise, and I just sat with Christina for a little bit. We prayed with her. I held her hands and she apologized because they were dusty, but I said it was okay so we kept holding hands. I felt fake when I prayed, but when we were done, Christina was crying, and so were we. That doesn't usually happen.

We sat there for a minute longer in the dirt and I told her she reminded me of my grandma, who had the same wrinkles and strong hands. Then we had to leave. Christina was smiling when we left and headed deeper into the neighborhood. She didn't go straight back to work. She waved and remained seated for a little while. Arden and I sniffed and wiped our tears, trying to restore our default settings for the next house.

This work is hard. When I do it, I don't trust God because I want to or because "'tis so sweet to trust in Jesus." I trust God because if I don't, I won't do it at all.

I think trusting God doesn't mean things feel comfortable and in control. I still slog from house to house and feel awkward. But sometimes, I can't wait for God to speak to me. I just have to start talking or hugging or sitting. And I know that despite or because of my action, God will show up. Even if I think I'm fake, I'm real.

July 18
Mzuzu, Malawi

Tomorrow we are hiking up to the top of a mountain with the youth group and worshipping on top. I have to preach. It's going to be a mountaintop experience.

I was half-heartedly planning when Arden sat down and told me to put my laptop away for once and just hang out. We chatted for a long time, and it was so much better than writing a sermon.

July 19
Mzuzu, Malawi

We are fasting lunch today, the day we have to hike up the mountain. I'm wearing my 1996 Atlanta Olympics Uncle Ben's Instant Fucking Rice t-shirt and my jeans and I am going to preach and I just don't want to. I'm dreading it. I'm not nervous. I just don't want to.

The mountain was more of a hill, but I'm protein-deprived and out of shape and grumpy enough that I found it exhausting. We're in a small clearing, sitting on chitenges.

I'm annoyed.

I'm annoyed at saying, "Amen!" all the time.

I'm annoyed at being told to lead song after song.

I'm annoyed at being told to dance for the Lord.

I'm annoyed at having to minister to people with bad theology.

I'm annoyed at being forced to be a performer.

I'm annoyed at the prosperity gospel. It's contaminated everything here. The songs say things like "With Jesus, everything is double!" and "I am a winner! I am a winner!" We go to church and pray for good jobs. We declare in the name of Jesus that we will be wealthy and triumphant, ignoring the fact that we worship a murdered, itinerant, Jewish peasant who was not a winner in any worldly sense.

This group we're with is always going on about how great we Racers are, because we gave up our wealth in America to come here.

"You'll get it all back and more," they tell us. "God is going to bless you with unimaginable riches as a reward for coming to minister to us." They make us stand up in church and tell the congregation that our ability to raise $15,500 means we are super powerful and smart. It's weird. I'm writing this during the time that's been set aside to pray for ourselves, for our future careers, if we're men, and future children, if we're women. But I'm not praying for those things.

One of the youth group members also said to me, "If you can't pray in tongues, just pretend you are."

Just, no.

July 20
Mzuzu, Malawi

Last night, as I was falling asleep, a bad feeling descended on me and I was suddenly afraid for my family. I started praying for them. I'm worried something happened, but we won't get internet for two more days.

Today I used the nastiest toilet of my life at a house church. The pastor warned me it was bad, but I said I didn't mind. It wasn't the dirty plywood door hanging on one hinge. It wasn't the flies. It wasn't the grime. It wasn't the wet toilet paper.

It was how, when you first looked in the hole, you saw a pale, yellow mound, and after a second, you realized the yellow was moving, because the yellow was thousands of maggots covering a mountain of feces, inches from the edge of the hole.

"I am not a slave to fear," I spoke over myself, "and I have very strong quads."

July 21
Mzuzu, Malawi
There was an email from Dad in my inbox that simply said:

"Chelsea, in case you haven't heard, Haley R. drowned
in a river in Germany, a devastating tragedy for everyone."

I broke down there, in the coffee shop. I sobbed and sobbed to
my team. I couldn't get a hold of my family.

Haley is a dear friend of my sister's and a beloved member of
my school and church community back in Washington. We weren't
close, but if we were the same age, we would have been. She's good
at everything and everyone loves her. She's kind, smart, confident,
and goes to Harvard. She's traveling and blogging around Europe
for the summer.

I don't know what to do. It's scary. It's random. I was so scared
something had happened to my family, I postponed logging into my
email for a long time. And there's that awful news. That's what's
going on in my community while I frolic around preaching about
nothing to people who don't need to hear it.

I don't get what's supposed to happen.

I read *A Grief Observed* by C. S. Lewis but it didn't work.

I feel like an asshole for being distracted and doing other stuff. I
feel like an imposter for being so sad when she wasn't my best friend.

It's scary because she was—already I have to say was, the present tense is no longer correct—brilliant. Gorgeous. Intelligent. Talented. Freakishly talented. Kate once said the only thing she wasn't
amazing at was singing, and even that was endearing.

I don't know what it makes me want to do.

Cry? I already did that in the coffee shop. The song "Lilongwe" was
playing and my team gathered around me and hugged me and asked
enough questions so I felt heard, but not so many I felt smothered.

I want revenge on what happened. I want to not be here any-more. I want to be home at Christmas. I want to be obnoxiously alive, so I can stave off what they say happens to everyone but what I don't believe can happen to me. If I live aggressively enough, learn enough, move enough, maybe death won't catch me.

But she is exactly the kind of person death doesn't catch, and it caught her.

Now what? Can I go to bed? I feel like God is telling me to rest, but I am not happy with God.

Dear God, fix things or piss off.

July 22
Mzuzu, Malawi
I can't evangelize. I can watch *New Girl* or cry, but I can't do ministry.

I am asking God for help, and I'm not saying that because I mean it or want it. I'm saying it from habit and numbness. Every-thing is painful, except prayer. Prayer is at least anesthetizing.

July 23
Mzuzu, Malawi
The thing is, I don't know what to do now. What do I do now?

I want to find upset Jesus. I'm going to go read the Bible and look for Him.

I'm reading the Gospel of Mark and so far, Jesus seems like a *guy*. A frazzled, stressed, blunt, astonishing guy who's impatient and tells both demons and the weather to shut up. He's always trying to get away but people stalk Him.

He's clearly come to serve. Tells people to do the same. Gets pissed when told to ignore kids or not heal. He always tries to keep Himself under wraps and I don't blame Him. They called that the Messianic Secret in my religion classes, but to me it reads as strong personal boundaries.

Okay, I finished Mark's Gospel.

That's a *weird* book.

That's what I learned: Jesus is a big weirdo! Of course I've read it before, but... weird. One of my professors once said it's the gospel as told by a guy at a dive bar.

"Okay, so right then, they're like on this boat, right, and then it's all stormy, and right then, right then, right then..."

The whole book is bizarre. I argue and doubt and question, but to see the story of the guy I agonize over? Things don't match up: He doesn't play my mind games. He talks and moves and heals and dies and disappears. I grew up wearing "What Would Jesus Do?" bracelets and I'm trekking around the world mimicking a man and a savior I don't even know.

I went to read it to find angry Jesus, what He does when He's upset, and I found out. He creates. He doesn't destroy. His wrath leads to restoration, like when He's pissed at the haters for not wanting Him to heal the guy's hand, and in that anger He brings justice, not devastation.

Create things. That's what to do with death. Get revenge on it by making and remaking.

Today I've been less troubled in general. The news doesn't feel new anymore, but it's hellish, because that means I don't think of Haley and what happened. I hate that this has happened. I *hate* it. Now, I'm afraid something will happen. Anything bad could happen, to anyone, at any time. My heart is broken and all of us are going to die.

I don't like seeing *Haley* and *death* in the same sentence. Those words don't go together. I want the words separated. I want to insert punctuation marks to protect Haley from death.

I second guess every little shit sermon I've given. I can't say anything right now. How am I supposed to preach on John 11, where Jesus says, "I am the Resurrection," after this? How can I say that God works everything out for good? How I can I trust that the gospel is big enough for this?

I need more than God just *being* with me. I need God to give me all the stuff I want: health, safety, sex, money, love, happiness. If God doesn't give me what I want, what do I get from this relationship? "Eternal life," they say. But I don't see that. I see death.

July 25
Mzuzu, Malawi
I suppose things have been happening this month.

Bible study this month has been fun. We go to Rebecca's house and eat lots of baked goods and she's a riot.

Jayce taught me how to smack gum and now I can do it really loudly. We ate sugarcane in the covered bed of a pickup on the way home from Bible study the other night and smacked gum together.

There have been more epic services with dancing and matching clothes and children climbing all over us and smiling and praise and power and chitenges and nsima.

Yesterday a bunch of us went to Prince Edward's maize fields to harvest them. It was nice. The field was endless and dry and prickly and I didn't pray for a single stranger. I had my headphones in and went off by myself.

July 27
Mzuzu, Malawi
I'm sort of sad to leave. This is a good place. Good people. Tragic month, though.

I did like Mzuzu Coffee Den a lot. There are artists outside who make bracelets and carvings. I commissioned a lot of wooden keychains for my family from one and bought a painting of elephants against a green sky from another.

And I liked the local market. We bought more chitenges there.

Tonight, I instigated the funniest team time. I made us put on a shadow puppet show and then I made us all squeeze into Jason's tent for no reason. I haven't laughed that hard in a long time.

July 28
Mabuya Camp again in Lilongwe, Malawi
I learned Oak will be together for another month (which I'm happy for) and that we're at an orphanage again in August. I just think of El Salvador... flashbacks of El Salvador. No, no, no, not that again.

The bus ride here from Mzuzu wasn't as long as I expected... I mean, it was, but five or six or seven or whatever hours means nothing now. It was a success because we didn't break down or spend the night anywhere or plummet from a cliff.

July 29
Lilongwe, Malawi
Resilience doesn't mean not experiencing things fully. I realized that today in our team meeting, when I said I was tired of ministry, worn out from grieving, and wanting to go home—and those are just the main things.

That's a lot to be struggling with, yet I said in the same breath, "I'm happy. I'm content. I'm at home."

I am full of joy and that is from God.

July 30
Lilongwe, Malawi
I guess we narrowly missed another riot today when we were out, but we're "safe" if we stay here. A month ago, I didn't care at all about some riot, and now I'm terrified.

A month ago, I didn't think death was real. And now, with Haley, and the ever-increasing sketchiness of the Race, I see that I'm mortal. I'm turning fearful. When things go wrong with travel or there's a riot nearby, I'm not just inconvenienced. I'm scared for my life. Haley's death infuses the days with fear. I don't want to worry, but now I know that bad things happen to everyone, everywhere, whenever.

July 31
Mzuzu, Malawi

Let me say for the record that I'm very afraid of going to Mozambique. There are former Racers at this hostel and expats with tricked-out Jeeps who've been there and they just talk about bus accidents, unrest, crime, corruption, and malaria.

I'm scared of bus accidents. I know we're not safe. People fall, cars crash. What if tomorrow is the last day? I feel like something horrible will happen. I'm praying for protection.

Tomorrow we leave. Yes, I'm scared. But I don't need to listen to it. The devil knows that this is going to be a bitchingly sweet month and is trying to get me down. The devil won't get me down. I'll have trouble but Jesus can overcome it. I'm trying to pump myself up. I'll blog:

Hi funky readers! Today we're leaving Lilongwe, Malawi, at 6:00 a.m. to travel to our *eighth* country, Mozambique! Yay! I'm not scared! Please pray for C Squad as we face bus boredom, a bureaucratic border crossing, potential delays, and potholes... and minor squabbles... and insufficient protein... and nausea... and death.

This month, Team Oak will be serving at a boys' home outside the port city of Beira. I don't know exactly what to expect, but what little I've heard suggests that this is going to be a wonderful month! I'll keep you posted! Hopefully it won't be like El Salvador when I was so sweaty, I lost my mind and my butt crack chafed!

STILL COUNTRY 7: NO-ZAMBIQUE

In which I do not go to Mozambique.

August 1
Blantyre, Malawi
We aren't in Mozambique.

August 4
Blantyre, Malawi
We left Mzuzu on Monday and traveled south to Lilongwe to prepare for the complicated process of traveling to Mozambique on Wednesday. In an effort to get us across safely, Cody and Kim spent an extra few days at the embassy, double checking our visas and filling out stacks of paperwork. On Friday, finally, we were cleared to leave for the border. Forty-one visas were pasted in each of our passports.

The bus ride to the border took about eight hours, which wasn't too bad. But the vehicle's floors were dusty and its seats were hard and straight-backed, and most of the cushions had long since detached from their frames. By the end of the ride, the center aisle was littered with linoleum and staple-gunned cushions.

We drove through a bustling market. Heaps of secondhand clothes were for sale on the ground, and canopies with sugarcane skeletons were strewn about in front of a bright green building on which had been painted GRAPH OF GOD.

When we were close to Mozambique, we found ourselves in green valleys. Mountains rose all around us, and the land was lush with trees and fruit. Dirty corrugated metal roofs dotted the fields.

We ditched the bus at the Malawi border. The plan was to take our luggage off and cross into Mozambique on foot, then meet up with a church contact who had organized our rides from there. After filling out forms that allowed us to exit Malawi, we loaded up and walked several hundred yards across a bridge, into Mozambique.

For three hours we waited outside customs. Our leaders turned in the applications and notarized invitations on church letterheads and fees. The rest of us sat on the steps, waiting for entry stamps.

We watched other people glide across the border on bikes. It grew colder and darker. We put on sweatshirts. We made sandwiches for dinner. We peed in bushes. A leader periodically emerged from the office and urged us to pray before disappearing inside.

At six o'clock the border closed and we were informed that we would not be allowed into Mozambique. They told us that in the previous week, the country had changed its entry requirements, and our paperwork was now unacceptable. I'm not clear on all the details, but I know that our invitations needed a signature from Religious Affairs in Maputo. Also, everything needed to be in Portuguese.

We had no choice but to walk back over the border to Malawi. The Malawian border had also closed for the night, and the few remaining employees told us that they wouldn't allow us back into the country.

Our bus had been gone for hours, so we assumed we'd have to spend the night there.

"But you cannot spend the night," said a guard. "Since you already received an exit stamp, you are under the control of Mozambique, and they are responsible for you."

"But Mozambique won't allow us in, so we need to be back in Malawi," we explained.

"But you can't go back to Malawi because you are not our responsibility anymore."

"But it is impossible for us to be in Mozambique now, so we need to get back into Malawi, or else we'll spend the night here at the border tonight."

"You cannot spent the night here at the border because you'll compromise our safety and yours. If you stay here we will have to chase you off."

"But there's nowhere for us to go. That is why we need you to let us back into Malawi."

"You cannot go back into Malawi. You have your exit stamp already."

This continued until one of our leaders, Bre, started flirting with the guard. She told him he had strong biceps and he was very good at his job until he called a customs official who had left for the night and asked him to let us back into Malawi. We called our bus, which was surely back in Lilongwe by then, and told the driver to turn around.

In the meantime, we compromised the border's safety and sprawled on the sidewalk in the dark. We ate more food. We were cold, and we huddled together between the two countries that didn't want us. How obnoxious we must have been, taking up all that space with our REI sleeping bags unfurled and untouchable American and Canadian passports at hand.

Kelsey, Nicole, and I hiked through some bushes behind the now dark customs office to relieve ourselves. I squatted in tall grass. I shined my headlamp straight ahead and it landed on two glowing eyes. The face underneath the eyes started barking fiercely, and the body underneath the face threw itself against the chain link fence that separated us.

"There's a dog!" we whisper-shrieked. But we couldn't move yet. Then, a shadowy figure approached us in the dark, brandishing a club.

Kelsey and Nicole were still in the bushes, so I ran up to him.

"Hello! Hello, and we are using the toilet here," I sputtered.

The guard said, "Oh."

I wanted to make absolutely sure he understood what was happening.

"Is that all right? My friends are *right there*." I pointed.

"Oh," he repeated. He didn't move.

"Is that all right?" I wanted him to go away.

"Yes." He didn't move.

"Thank you, sir," I said. I looked over. Kelsey and Nicole were pulling up their pants, stifling guffaws. The guard stood there and glared as we walked back to the sidewalk.

Relieved, we had an incredible view of the stars. The electricity was off for the night, which made us feel both vulnerable and awestruck.

I don't know if I have ever seen the Milky Way in the States, but we see it a lot here in Africa. Every time we see it, we tell one another, "That's the Milky Way! Do you see it?"

And we reply to one another, "Yes! I see it!"

Hours later, the necessary personnel appeared to cross out our Malawi exit stamps and our bus returned. We loaded our bags back on. It was a sleepy, cold two hours to the city of Blantyre, where a rogue World Race contact named Jarvis had arranged a place for us to crash.

I expected the ride to be over every time I saw a church, but it was church, church, church, and we kept driving by churches. We came to a tiny schoolhouse. We crowded into the classrooms, eight to a room, and slept, claustrophobic and exhausted.

The next couple days, we were stranded at the schoolhouse. We walked around town and talked to some people and sang some worship songs here and there. We didn't have anything else to do so some of us went and saw the Malawi Flames beat Benin in a football match and a lot of us had our iPhones stolen. At the schoolhouse, we watched movies and played with the neighborhood kids.

In my room, our sleeping pads were so close together that the monster of a scorpion living beneath them couldn't get up to threaten us. On Sunday, when we packed our pads away to move houses, I stepped on him. My first scorpion kill of the Race.

After two days, our contact Jarvis arranged for C Squad to move to the backyard of his mother's house, and that is where we are now. We're waiting to hear if Mozambique will let us in. Today or tomorrow, there will be a meeting in Maputo where they will decide whether we can enter. Until they do, we are stranded in Blantyre.

But the house is beautiful and it has a backyard that people rent out for weddings. It has a shower and a kitchen and a living room with a big screen TV that was playing *Love Comes Softly* when we arrived last night. It's a good place to wait.

We're hoping the Mozambican government will let us into the country so we can head to our new ministry sites this week. Team Oak has a fantastic month ahead of us at a boys' home near the city of Beira, and we cannot wait to meet our new ministry hosts!

But for now, we are in Blantyre all together, waiting for No-zambique to give us a yes.

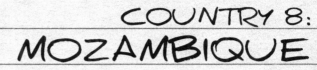

COUNTRY 8:
MOZAMBIQUE

In which I live under mango trees,
am assumed to be carrying a flash
drive of Phil Collins music,
and witness a miracle.

August 7

Beira, Mozambique

Getting stuck between Malawi and Mozambique was a hassle. It was a little freaky. I thought for a moment we would get shot peeing in the bushes. But we worked it out. We kept our spirits high enough. It was an adventure.

Getting to Beira, however, just sucked.

On Monday, August 4, after four days in Blantyre, half of C Squad's paperwork somehow fell into place, and Oak was one of the three teams ordered to pack and be ready in the morning to enter Mozambique via a different border.

At 7:00 a.m. the next day, 21 of us crowded into two 15 passenger vans with 42 backpacks. The ride to the border was only two hours and we were in Mozambique before we knew it. Just like that.

We exchanged high fives and thought the worst was over! From here we had six hours to go to Gorongosa. There, the other two teams would stay with a South African missionary couple, and Team Oak would drive another three hours to a boys' home outside Beira. We would be there by dinnertime. It would be easy.

But we weren't, and it wasn't.

In my van were 17 of us and some of our luggage. The van had 12 seats. The other van with the other four people and most of our bags could only go 30 miles an hour or it would overheat, so we had to drive slowly too.

The police saw that we were foreigners and they stopped our vans over and over. They made us get out and show them our passports and yellow fever vaccination cards, trying to find something to fine us for.

In addition to the van overheating and the cops stopping us, we kept taking breaks so the drivers could stretch their legs. We'd get out and pee, and ask how long it would be until we reached Gorongosa (surely, any minute, we thought, as the shadows lengthened and the day cooled). And every time we asked, we were told the same thing:

"Three more hours."

"Three more hours."

"Three more hours."

We weren't in Gorongosa at 3:00 p.m. or Beira at dinnertime. We were crawling through Mozambique, sealed into a humid, nauseous van from breakfast time until 7:00... the next morning.

Around midnight, our vans stopped on a dark, dusty road. The only light came from a small restaurant across the street. The driver told us we had to stay there a while because the police didn't want anyone driving on the next stretch of road until morning. Too tired and miserable to protest, we slumped onto each other and closed our eyes.

A drunk man came up to our van. He introduced himself as Nito and told us we were silly to try to drive at this time of night. "Why are you going to Gorongosa?" he demanded. "Park and spend the night here."

"We're just going to keep driving as soon as possible," said Bre.

"No, you can't do that," protested Nito. "It's time to sleep!"

"Thank you, but we'll stay here and be ready to leave."

"There are *animals* on the road," he insisted.

"Animals?" I pictured lions and giraffes, out at night together being thugs, keying cars and slashing tires.

"Yes, there are so many animals. This car is no good. You need to park it and use a different car." Nito was hell-bent on getting us all to... well, I'm not sure exactly what he wanted us to do. He didn't work for a hotel, or a parking garage, or taxi service. In fact, he worked in medicine.

"I'm a nurse," he said. He reached in the car and pinched Bre's butt.

While some of the more patient passengers humored Nito and talked about the animals and asked if he knew Jesus and explained that no, we weren't going to stay in this place to minister, thanks anyway, I was past the point of manners. I sat in the back and pressed my forehead into the seat in front of me.

My gaze drifted downward and I discovered that we didn't have to go down that scary road to see wildlife: there were animals at our feet! I somehow hadn't noticed in the last 12 hours that the wall and floor of the van were covered with cockroaches. Most of them were nestling in a busted pink wall speaker. I thought about crushing them with my hand, water bottle, bag of chips... until I looked on the floor and saw a stray length of sugarcane. Perfect. I stabbed at them and they fled, taking refuge in cracks and crevices under the seats.

After realizing this stop was no brief potty break and we really would have to wait for the police to let us drive on, I crossed the street to the little restaurant, which was still open at 2:00 a.m., where Nicole and Kelsey were napping on the stoop. I joined them, lying partly under a plastic table. We were lying there, not caring if we were being rude or gross, when a tall, skinny man stepped out and looked at us and said something.

"Okay?" I asked, pointing at ourselves, lolling in the doorway of his establishment.

"*Sim*," he replied, and disappeared. We sighed with relief and relaxed, all three of us using Nicole's backpack as a pillow.

A moment later, he returned with a big bamboo mat. He motioned for us to stand up. We rose and watched the mat unfurl with a snap and float to the ground. We didn't know "thank you" in Portuguese yet, so we said it in English and fell asleep for two hours.

When we were allowed to drive again, we woke and saw that the restaurant had closed but our friend was sitting on the porch, keeping an eye on us. When we left, he stood, rolled up the mat, and disappeared.

We drove and drove and drove and finally reached Gorongosa, an area known for being war-torn and malaria-ridden. Rupert, one of the South African missionaries, drove us in two batches in the back of his pickup truck for an hour on a nasty, bumpy road to his house out in the bush, which was made of tarps. He was white and scruffy and had strange, benevolent eyes.

His wife, Ruth, gave us tea and coffee while breakfast heated up over a fire. It was supposed to have been yesterday's dinner. In one pot was rice. In the other was springbok.

The springbok stew was flavorful and tender and gamey, and Ruth had added chunks of carrots, potatoes, and cabbage. Peppercorns and star anise stuck in my teeth. It was comfort food hearty enough to soothe the exhaustion of a grueling 24-hour drive across the border and through the wilderness of Nito's animals and down a 30-mile dirt road in the bed of a pickup. Satisfied, I spread my chitenge on the hard, cracked earth and slept.

It felt like a night passed at Ruth and Rupert's house but it was only several hours later that Rupert loaded his pickup again to take Team Oak to Beira. The bed of the truck was full of luggage, but four of us had to ride atop it and I frantically called, "It's mine! I'll sit there!"

It was a long, cramped drive, but the wind provided joy. There's something objectively wonderful about riding in the back of a pickup truck. Bre and I sat with our long, travel-weary legs sticking out the back and our butts going numb, and Heidi and Jason perched on top of the bags.

On the previous day's hellish bus ride, cops had pestered us constantly, but today, no one halted our progress. I had chuckled when Ruth put her hands on our knees as the car started and prayed: "Lord, let no one see their white skin," but it must have worked.

It had been a long enough time since the springbok stew to eat again. I opened a can of Bashew's raspberry soda and a package of dry ramen noodles I'd brought from Malawi. My confidence bolstered by the ease of this last leg of our journey, I gnawed open the curry flavored spice packet and sprinkled it on the block of noodles. Most of the powder swirled away on the wind, which I found romantic.

Yes, I had just spent a solid day on a cramped, cockroachy, carsick ride that had me hating the World Race. Yes, we were exhausted. But this was a new day. I was riding in the bed of a pickup, eating dry noodles and drinking sweet soda and laughing with my friends. My headband—or was it Heidi's?—blew off in the wind. All was well.

The last 48 hours were such horrific travel, long travel, dangerous travel—in fact, "travel" is too kind a word for whatever it was we were doing when we were puking in those hot vans, squatting over maggoty toilets, squishing roaches against seats with our knees, getting delayed in the middle of the night, sleeping outside that shop, driving for hours and hours and hours and hours and hours—but *boom*, through smoking fields and rooibos tea and raspberry sodas, here we are in Mozambique.

Here we are at a commune of treehouses and teenage boys and one bearded, kind, smart man from Wyoming named Matthew, who is our ministry host. He drinks from his wedding wine glasses in memory of his bride, who was killed by a water buffalo on their honeymoon, and devotes himself to her dream of building a home for Mozambican boys. He makes the boys work hard and play hard. Build a ping pong table! Irrigate the garden! Everyone go swimming! Take the day off and play football!

This is a haven of coconuts and kittens and big, big beers that Matthew won't be guilted into declining. There is a library full of books I love to study: dusty Greek New Testaments, the Zohar, and the Talmud. They are tucked in between guides to butchering and carpentry and farming.

I don't even know what we did to get *into* this country, but now we are here. We are nestled into this mango tree heaven—they go up forever, and we can climb and climb and climb them—and there are smashed pottery mosaics in the ground and a rickety Seussian water tower to climb, and strange livestock on the volleyball court.

I was so afraid that we wouldn't make it here. But we *did*, and now that we're here, it's like we've dropped off the face of the earth in the best possible way.

Leave It All

August 9
Beira, Mozambique

Heather is a long-term missionary who has lived here a while. She's kind and stern and funny. Courtney, Heidi, and I sleep in her colorful house in a spare room where our mattresses touch and our blue and purple mosquito nets sag under the weight of the many cats that climb them and nestle on top. We wake up with them in our faces. We watch movies on our laptops and cuddle in the mild heat and we know each other so well we don't need to be polite or rude. This easy community is what'll make a missionary of me.

We have real shower stalls but no plumbing. Thankfully Heather's British so she has a kettle for tea. We use it to add hot water to the cold buckets.

We eat oatmeal for breakfast and ants get in it. The ants are so small, we don't pick them out. I've had so much oatmeal this year. I might eat ants later in life but I don't see how I will ever enjoy oatmeal again.

My feet have been dirty for three months. I barely wear shoes anymore. I don't have a single piece of clothing that isn't in bad shape. I think I look grand. This month we don't have to evangelize and preach so we can get dirty all we want.

The boys run all over the place. They each have their own jobs: caring for the animals, building tables, landscaping, gardening, cooking. They're always climbing the water tower but I don't. It scares me, I guess.

On Mondays, local widows come and the boys serve them food and fill bags of rice.

For dinner we eat rice and beans and greens cooked in fresh coconut milk.

Portuguese sounds like blurry Spanish.

Country 8: Mozambique

August 15
Beira, Mozambique

I've just discovered the Beatles.

Matthew plays music on the speakers every morning to wake us, and today, it was "Here Comes the Sun." The riff drew me out of a dream, tickled me through the mosquito net, and I woke up with Heidi and Courtney next to me and the pet cats lurking nearby and the roosters crowing outside.

August 17
Beira, Mozambique

Last year, a gang broke into this complex with machetes and World Racers were staying here in their tents, and it was scary and the people almost attacked, but Matthew had a gun so that scared them off. That's why they have guard dogs here and that's why we sleep inside.

But today, we found planks of wood up against the wall, on the inside, so that if you were to get on top of the outer wall, you could walk down them like ramps. Heather said someone who wanted to do us harm must have put them there, and she rolled her eyes and put them aside. She just seemed annoyed, but seeing those boards scared me.

One of my sports bras has been stolen from the line.

August 18
Beira, Mozambique

Finally replying to emails.
To a friend from college:

> Hey friend! It *has* been a while, huh? Time's so weird for me...
>
> Well, we *hadn't* seen any snakes in Africa... until last week. This last week, I've seen three. Here, you say "cobra"

when you mean a generic snake. And when you mean a cobra like we think of a cobra, you say "ninja." So this week, I've seen one cobra and two ninjas. They slither out of nowhere, and as soon as we spot them, the dogs start barking and the boys all grab two by fours and start yelling from a safe distance. Then Matthew, the guy who runs this place, bashes the snake's head in with a crowbar and lets the kids play with the twitching body.

I asked Matthew if a ninja bite would kill you, and he said, "Probably not, but you'd wish it would."

The morning is for working and the afternoon is for playing. There's always some project going on, and Matthew has a lot of construction experience and he uses it to teach the boys here, mostly orphaned local kids, skills like carpentry, welding, etc. The boys do all their own cooking, which is impressive, since it's some of the best food we've had on the Race. He lets them make cake and doughnuts, they're allowed off the property to see friends or go to church as they wish, and every night we make a *giant* pot of popcorn and have a movie night. Last night we watched *Dr. Who*, the night before was *How to Train Your Dragon*… it's a great way to unwind every night and hang out with the kids and help them learn English.

On Fridays, we spend the whole day making bread to eat on Saturday so we don't have to cook on the Sabbath. Friday nights, the adults here have wine and cheese and listen to a podcast done by a Jew, a Christian, and some guy whose religious views no one knows. They discuss the week's Torah portion, and then we talk about it. Then on Saturday, we do nothing. Last Sabbath I was on a sofa all day long, reading, asking Matthew questions about his theology, and studying from a Hebrew textbook I found…

To Mom and Dad:

Hey, just a couple other quick things I could use from home! First, if you have time and room, could you pick up a mosquito net from REI? I'm wishing I brought one! If you can, get one that hangs from a single point, and is for a twin size bed. Get the one that packs down the smallest. And if there's a choice of colors, I'd like white: easier to see bugs that way.

But if you have to choose what to bring, I'd rather have clothes because I can buy nets most places. Maybe we can try to FaceTime next week or something during our debrief... but I need a t-shirt and maybe a tank top... could you look through my stuff and see if there are any tank tops that would be good in really hot weather and aren't too shlubby? And for a t-shirt... is there something light and kinda baggy? And casual and old is okay. Let me know what you see!

And finally, a dress. What dresses do I have that would be good in hot weather? Something quick drying, knee length or so?

Sorry if this is a lot of stuff. Tell me if you can't fit everything because these aren't all super essential. Did you get everything else on the list? Like my swimsuit and laptop charger?

To another friend:

...I'm on the second story of what is almost a tree house. Tonight's dinner is beer and popcorn. I am drinking Manica, *un cervejas de Moçambique*. Every night, the boys watch a movie, and tonight's is *Swat*, a cop film, and I'm both bored and stressed out by it, so I'm not really paying attention. One of the boys, Lucas, is going through my phone looking for games. There are seven dogs here and a bazillion cats, and most of them are on the couches in here. People are on plastic chairs and the floor.

Matthew projects the movie on a white sheet on the open-air second story of this building, so you can watch from inside where we are or from the picnic tables below. He has cool ideas like that. He's altered the sink upstairs to make it easier to fill water balloons, which he pelts with terrifying precision at whoever's preparing food in the kitchen below.

This morning at breakfast, a cow licked my elbow (at least someone can) and then I shared my Sabbath breakfast of flatbread, jam, and iced coffee in a beer bottle with her.

August 19
Beira, Mozambique
Arden and I climbed the water tower at sunset and had a nice talk.

August 20
Beira, Mozambique
Tomorrow, Bre has to get to Caia to meet up with the other squad leaders. Caia is a few hours away and she needs two people to accompany her. Jayce volunteered because he's a kind human, but I was asked to go and only grudgingly agreed. I'm scared of getting in a wreck.

The driver is Pastor Archie, a guy we just bumped into around town who is not a real pastor. I'm nervous about riding with him for eight hours. It terrifies me that nothing is certain.

August 21
Beira, Mozambique
I'm back from the drive to Caia. It *sucked*. Here's why.

1. Pastor Archie's friend Mark came with us and rode shotgun. Mark just married, and we congratulated him and asked if he had photos of his wife. He produced one of them in their

wedding clothes before a cheap blue background, the kind they use for school pictures. Mark and his wife looked serious and formal, except Mark was reaching across her body and clutching her boob with one hand. "Oh, how nice," said Bre, in the voice she uses when something isn't nice.

2. We drove through Gorongosa, which used to be a lush national park but has been ravaged by war. There were vast riverbeds that had totally dried up.

3. Pastor Archie kept saying, "Buy my country! Buy it and fix it up!" We laughed politely at first, assuming it was a joke we didn't get, but he wouldn't stop saying it and we started to think he was somehow serious.

4. Pastor Archie gestured to a great plain and told us that the vice president was hiding out there somewhere.

5. Jayce had some cookies, and Pastor Archie asked for one, so Jayce gave him the box, and then Pastor Archie ate all the cookies.

6. Pastor Archie and Mark wanted to listen to music, so they asked us three if we had *a flash drive of Phil Collins music*. Specifically Phil Collins. They didn't ask for anything else. They turned on the radio when we said no. Why the fuck would anyone just have a flash drive of Phil Collins?

7. Bre and I had to pee, so Pastor Archie pulled onto the shoulder in a very flat area. There were bushes in the distance so we walked to them. As we walked back, Pastor Archie took photos of us.

8. Pastor Archie stopped the car over a bridge in the heart of Gorongosa and made us get out and stand against the rail and hold hands and take a photo together. He made me so uncomfortable, I tried to lower my center of gravity and get heavy, in case he decided to push us off.

9. Pastor Archie asked Bre and me if we were married, and we said, "Well, no," and he was creepy and asked when we

would get married. Bre said she had a boyfriend and talked about him. I tried to invent my pretend boyfriend but the only person coming to my mind was my brother.

10. The ride to Caia took six hours, which was twice as long as they told us. It wasn't surprising, but when we finally arrived and Bre met the other squad leaders and was on her way, Jayce and I just wanted to get back. But Pastor Archie and Mark wanted to eat dinner. We went to a restaurant and Mark drank a beer. Jayce and I didn't care about keeping the conversation moving anymore so we just sat in silence.

11. We bought gas and there was a man there filling canisters. Pastor Archie said that it's common to buy all the gas so the station doesn't have any left, and then sell it at a premium. Already it was three times the price as in Beira.

12. We drove back, and I was so tired and so miserable at how creeped out I felt around Pastor Archie and Mark. I wanted to put my head on Jayce's shoulder and fall asleep, but there was an empty middle seat between us. We slumped toward each other, glaring forward at the road. I kept telling myself that it would all be funny someday.

13. We were *so close* to being back when Pastor Archie stopped by a lone vendor, late at night, selling tomatoes, and took forever to buy a sack of them.

14. We lost a day of ministry. We spent it on two creepy men, and a long-ass drive.

August 22
Beira, Mozambique
I hated spending yesterday in the car instead of with my team. But now I want to throw myself into everything that's going on here—I want to *build* these brick ping pong tables, I want to *walk* to the market with the boys to buy coconut and tomatoes and greens for the rice—last night it wasn't home or Thailand or some distant

cosmopolitan life I dreamt of while I slouched in the backseat with Jayce. It was *here*, under the rustling mangoes of a compound on the edge of Beira, running around with teenagers and livestock, laying bricks, talking theology, watching *Dr. Who* on a dirty white sheet, with Team Oak, who lives together so easily, whom I love.

For team time today, I had us sit around a concrete picnic table in the bright shade and say what we loved about each other.

I don't want this life to go away.

August 23
Beira, Mozambique
Heather has a friend named Jeremy, a redhead from Brazil. He is charming. When we met, he kissed my cheek. Most action I've had all year.

There is WiFi here, but a previous team of Racers caused this place to get fined 800 dollars over their normal bill. So Matthew gave us an internet stick and that's all we get. We haven't used much of it at all. We have two gigabytes for the whole team but we don't really use it. We're not supposed to blog this month because we don't want to draw attention to ourselves anymore anyway.

August 24
Beira, Mozambique
Leaving Beira tomorrow, though I won't believe *that* till it happens.

I'll miss this place and it's sad that it seems like the one place I'll never really be *able* to come back to, since it was such a nightmare getting here. I will treasure this month.

August 25
Beira, Mozambique
Driving to Caia today to meet the rest of the squad and Rupert and Ruth. The other half of C Squad never even made it into Mozambique. They just spent two months in Malawi. Their paperwork never

went through, and they've been in Blantyre, Malawi all August, staying at Jarvis's mother's house like we did for those few days.

If I'd stayed on B Squad and stayed obsessed with my route, I'm sure I would have been disappointed many times over by now. I'm so glad I switched.

But I had a bad attitude this morning about leaving. It took 90 minutes just to find a public minibus heading to Caia. We were crammed in there, four to a three-person row, with all this office furniture strapped to the roof of the vehicle. I was in the back corner of the back seat. I had the window open for air, which invited the street vendors. A man said something in Portuguese through the window and I turned away from him.

"No, thank you, sir." said Heidi.

"We're getting hassled," hissed Courtney.

The man didn't leave. He kept talking into the van.

"I don't want chips," I said to myself. "I don't want a razor. I don't want soap. I don't want a fan. I don't want apples. I don't want juice or pop."

"Do you want toothpaste?" Heidi asked.

"No."

"Colgate?"

"No Colgate." I started to smile in spite of myself which irritated me more but also made me laugh at myself. I looked out the window: the man was now brandishing a box of pastries.

"I kind of want one of those muffins, but I'm not going to admit it."

"Hey, what's on top of this bus?" asked Heidi.

"A freezer," said Jason.

"A *freezer?*" Courtney and I said together.

"A chest freezer."

"Are we gonna tip over, Jason?" I asked, gnawing at my chipped, dirty nail polish.

"No, we're not." Courtney rubbed my back.
"I'm afraid of tipping over."

August 26
I don't know where, Mozambique
This is nuts—

August 27
Cape Maclear, on the shore of Lake Malawi, Malawi
We are here. Fucking finally. Yesterday was a day I'll never forget. Yesterday, all my guts *knew* God was with us.

On August 25th, my team left our ministry and the town of Beira and traveled to Gorongosa. There, we waited for an hour on a busy street corner near a market.

Then, Rupert arrived in his pickup and drove us 200 kilometers to Caia. Rupert, remember, is the South African pastor we met at the beginning of the month, whose wife Ruth had served us springbok stew upon our entry into Mozambique. I sat in the back of the truck and ate dry ramen noodles and watched the sun set.

When it was late, we came to a church and met the teams that had been with Rupert and Ruth all month. We set up our tents and had three hours to sleep. I didn't unpack anything but my sleeping bag.

Now, this was how we planned to get to Lake Malawi—and I say planned with a smirk, because traveling in Africa has never gone to plan—by dinnertime the next day:

1. On Tuesday, August 26th, a truck would come at 4:30 in the morning to take us to the Zambezi River.
2. From there, a ferry would carry us to yet *another* car on the other side.

3. That other car would drive us to the border of Malawi and Mozambique.
4. Once in Malawi, Jarvis, the Malawian pastor whose mother had hosted us in Blantyre when we couldn't get into Mozambique, would meet us and drive us back to Blantyre.
5. We'd reunite with the half of C Squad that had been in Malawi all month in Blantyre.
6. Then, we would take buses to Cape Maclear on the shores of Lake Malawi, where we would swim with the fishies and worship Jesus for a few days.

It was supposed to take 12 hours.

First of all, the 4:30 a.m. ride stood us up.

We woke at 3:45 and packed our tents in the bleary dark and waited and it didn't come.

Rupert ran around like a chicken with its head cut off looking for a different ride. To pass the time, I drank water and Deborah showed me a video of herself actually cutting a chicken's head off.

Jayce decided to start recording everything that went wrong. Thanks to his foresight, I know for a fact these times are right.

At 6:30, Rupert found a man with a flatbed truck who was willing to drive us to the Zambezi. There were 19 of us in the bed of the truck, plus our daypacks, water jugs, guitars and my mandolin, and food.

"What time do you guys think we'll get to our debrief?" asked Heidi as we bounced along.

"Everyone take bets," said Kori. "What time are we gonna get to debrief? I vote 12:30 a.m."

"By two o'clock—" someone ventured.

"I vote tomorrow, 6:00 a.m."

"We're supposed to be there at 6:00 p.m."

The drive to the Zambezi lasted 90 minutes and ended when the road met river. We were told that this was the ferry landing. We saw no ferry, but someone said it would come at 10:00 a.m., which was in two hours. So we sat behind the truck in the shade.

Team Oak had planned to buy food in Caia for this day of travel, but we never had the chance. So now we were past Caia and we only had six 48-hour-old fried egg sandwiches on white rolls with lettuce. With two hours and our stomachs to kill, we unzipped the putrid communal tote bag and studied them.

"It was sort of chilly last night," we rationalized. "They'll be fine."

The lettuce was limp and black. The green had seeped into the cheese, egg, and bread. We were grossed out so we peeled off the lettuce and threw it on the ground. We took bites of the sandwiches. I showed mine to people and asked if they thought it was okay, and they said, "Well, I don't know. I wouldn't." I tried to eat it anyway, but the egg tasted like a bad idea and after a few bites it joined the lettuce on the ground.

It was getting hot. We sat in the dirt and stacked round pebbles on top of each other and discussed "travel day humor," the phenomenon that occurs when you are so worn out from all the moving and waiting and logistical nightmares that you start laughing at everything without finding anything funny.

Like the banana Jason ate that was so big it was almost two bananas.

Or drawing eyes on our chins and hanging upside down.

Or the suggestion, "There's a bridge over there. Let's just walk to Malawi instead."

The ferry didn't come at 10:00 a.m.

At 11:30, word came that it had run out of diesel and would not come at all.

The only other way across the Zambezi was over the Dona Ana Bridge, a train trestle that on its completion in 1934 was the longest in Africa at over three and a half kilometers.

Let's walk to Malawi, indeed.

We drove to the bridge in the trucks, bracing ourselves to walk over two miles with our sixty pounds of luggage. But when we arrived, there was a fleet of bike taxis waving at us. Turns out that Rupert had struck up a conversation with a man named James at the ferry landing, and James had arranged for 20 cyclists to pedal our big packs over the bridge, plus Laura, who had a bum foot. We would walk with our smaller items and meet them at the other side.

Here, we said goodbye to Rupert and Ruth, the guardians of our time in Mozambique. We would not have gone anywhere without them. We hugged them and thanked them for taking care of us and going out of their way to keep us moving on.

They said, "Some of you we will not see before we get to heaven, but hopefully, some of you, we will see again soon."

We parted ways, again.

How many times we have parted ways this year.

We walked.

"Tonight," said Deborah, "we will eat food that we didn't cook, and sleep in a bed, and take hot showers."

"Amen," someone declared.

There were officers patrolling the bridge and they stopped us. One asked Jayce for money. Another told Deborah to open her backpack. We showed him our passports and he glared at them.

The officer who was digging through Deborah's backpack found a bag of pills and started interrogating her.

"It's ibuprofen," she said, weary. "It's all labeled, but you can confiscate it. I don't care. Take it." After a few minutes, they gave it back to her and let her go.

I wasn't happy about the walk, but it was beautiful on the river, under that hot blue sky. Through the gaping holes in the bridge we could see the land below us. Motorcycles passed us on the right. I was carrying my daypack, my mandolin, and a bunch of bananas. I ate one to lighten my load and threw another one into the Zambezi because it was mushy and going black, like the lettuce.

When we reached the other side at noon, we found our packs stacked neatly near some ant hills. The spectacle had drawn yet more policemen.

The chief was there, straddling a janky motorcycle and telling us that he wanted to check all our packs and passports. We told them to go ahead and please get started, because we were in a hurry.

We should have been at the border by 10:00 a.m. and in Blantyre by 2:00 p.m. It was now almost 1:00 p.m. and we were still barely out of Caia. When the chief said he wanted to inspect our stuff, I started to wonder if we'd even make it to the border, which closed at 6:00 p.m.

We waited for close to an hour at the end of the bridge, sitting on logs and getting bitten by ants and burning in the sun. The chief and his officers were insisting that we go to the station to have our things inspected since they didn't want to do it out in the open, and we told them that if they wanted to do that, they'd have to provide the transportation, since, for the third time that day, our scheduled ride had failed to show up.

The police seemed reluctant about going through the trouble of finding us transportation, so they hemmed and hawed for a long time and we sat there and itched ourselves.

But then James appeared. I hadn't noticed, but he must have crossed the bridge with us. He took the police chief behind a tree and talked to him for a couple minutes. Then they came back holding hands and smiling and told us we didn't have to go to the station anymore.

So now we were free again, but we still didn't have a ride. That was when a tall, gruff, white South African man appeared. He had a beer in one hand.

He introduced himself as Conrad, a friend of James's.

"James told me you'd be needing rides to the border," he said. "I've got transportation."

"Okay!"

"Thank you!"

"Do you think we can make it to the border before it closes to-night?" we asked him.

"No chance," Conrad said.

He said that we were too conspicuous not to be bothered, that 30 miles on that appalling road would take too long, that the border itself would take hours to get through. He said we could stay with him that night and make the journey tomorrow. The leaders thanked him and declined, saying we would try to get to Malawi anyway. We were on a schedule and we were finished with this country.

But like I said, I was doubting we'd make it that day. A meal and a good night's sleep was starting to sound good.

Despite Conrad's advice, it was agreed that we'd try to cross the border that day, even though it was getting less likely by the minute. With the help of some local kids, we took our bags and walked to the trucks Conrad had arranged for us.

Guess what kind of transportation it was. You probably won't.

Conrad has lived in Mozambique on the Zambezi for years and works with a conservation program. He and James work for a croc-odile hatchery. Whenever Conrad needs to transport crocodiles and their eggs to wherever it is people transport crocodiles and their eggs, he loads them into a special flatbed truck, outfitted for reptile transport with a wire and canvas cage built up around it.

I don't know how many crocodiles the truck can carry, but I can tell you that it snugly fits 19 standing adults and their luggage.

We were excited when Conrad told us it was a crocodile truck and when James agreed to drive but refused payment. After a day of being abandoned and overcharged by drivers, his generosity made us crinkle our eyes in delight.

The crocodile truck lurched forward to resume the ever-madder dash for the border.

One minute later, we stopped again. We rolled our eyes, assum-ing it was another police inspection.

But this time, it wasn't.

A blue cooler appeared in the bed of the truck, and then a man. "Hello, hello! I'm Patrick! I'm with Conrad and James," he said.

He was beaming. He was big and tall and had bare feet and one arm. He wore shorts and a blue, button-up, short-sleeved shirt, the right sleeve of which fluttered in the breeze.

With his left hand, he opened the cooler and any further introductions were drowned out by a collective gasp, followed by cheers, for inside the cooler were frosty Cokes, Sprites, Fantas, and Sparlettas, nestling in a bed of ice. Conrad and James must have seen how tired we were and called ahead to Patrick, who went and bought the drinks.

Time crunch or no time crunch, we needed something cold. We opened the banged-up glass sodas, and we chugged them and burped and smiled at this man, Patrick. We knew everything would be okay.

Patrick was strangely moved at the opportunity to refresh us. He kept laughing and shaking our hands and getting teary, like we had just given *him* the sodas.

"I've found the reason I'm here," he told us, over and over. "I've lived in Mozambique for years and I just found the reason I'm here: it's to help you!" When he said that, I knew that despite all the setbacks, God was showing up. If our delay was what let us meet Patrick, it was worth it.

Weak with gratitude and high on sugar and bolstered by his kindness, we shouted blessings at Patrick as we headed for that border.

It was 2:30 p.m.

We drove on in triumph. We laughed at our fortune. We worshiped and quoted Scripture because everything was going to be fine. We didn't care that some of us were standing for the long drive ahead, because it was still more comfortable than most, and we were going to Malawi tonight, where we would hang out on the lake for a week, and then we would fly to Thailand, and I would see my parents there, and I'd fly home in time for Christmas and start a career and marry and be famous and live happily ever after...

We drove one kilometer before we stopped again, and this time, it *was* the police. We were in front of the station.

They made us park out front and send representatives into the office. I waited in the truck while they asked what we were doing, who sent us, if we were married, what denominations we were, and what we had studied in school.

They took our passports. Numbers were copied. Stamps were inspected.

An hour later, we were still there and they wouldn't return our passports.

James decided to call Conrad and Patrick. Right away, the two men drove up in a dusty pickup. We were still in the crocodile truck and we stuck our fingers through the cage and waved. Patrick leapt from the passenger seat onto the orange earth. His bare feet sent up puffs of dust and his massive belly jiggled as he bounded toward us.

"*Do not worry!*" he bellowed. "God is with you and I am close behind!"

Patrick ran right into the chief's office. As soon as he was inside, we heard his jovial voice turn violent. He screamed at the officers. He swore at them and we were afraid he had lost control of himself. But when he emerged from the office, he was docile. He shrugged and grinned.

"It seems like this is not working!" he announced. "Usually it works when I do that! It seems you may be here quite a long time!"

He laughed and smiled and so did we, for his sake. But we were mad at the police, who had decided to wait for a "phone call" from "the authorities" before returning our passports and letting us go to the border.

There was no problem with our passports or paperwork. They just wanted to delay us and get some money. We didn't want to bribe them, but at this point we were willing to do anything. We offered to give them what we had, but it must not have been enough, because they refused.

So Patrick went back inside and tried threatening them.

"They will write about this on the *internet*! They will tell people not to go to Mozambique on Facebook and there will be no tourists! This is bad press for you! Do you want to be responsible for Mozambique losing its tourists?"

There was another spell of silence, and then he unleashed another barrage of profanity.

Again, he came out of the office smiling sheepishly, apologizing for cursing around so many Christian women.

"It seems you will be here a *very* long time!" he said.

We smiled weakly.

"But you are the reason I'm here," he repeated. "This must be why I came to Mozambique: to help you people, because *you've* been helping people! I'm so glad we met."

When yet another round of yelling proved unsuccessful, Patrick said we'd better pray, and we stood in a circle in front of the police office and prayed that they would let us go soon. Then we asked to pray for Patrick.

Patrick said he didn't deserve it.

"I drink too much, I swear too much, I've lost too many people because I'm a real baddie," he said. "I didn't lose this arm to a crocodile, you know. I lost it in a driving accident because I was drunk."

We kept telling him that we didn't care about all that and neither did God, and we prayed for him and blessed him. We kept telling him that we loved him and it didn't matter what he had done. We were happy to meet him, and he was happy to meet us.

Patrick suggested that the women all go ask to use the office's bathrooms. "That way, they'll understand you're human beings with needs and they can't just keep you here all night."

Our problem was actually the opposite: we were thirsty. We were almost out of water and carefully rationing what we had left. Patrick saw this and sent Conrad out on a mission. He returned with another cooler of ice cold water bottles for us. Again, no payment was accepted.

The question of our passports came up: if the police didn't return them to us, would we be willing to come back for them tomorrow?

"Hell no," we said.

Patrick went in the office again to tell them that "they absolutely will not leave without their documents," and then he came out again. He said, rather excitedly, "It seems to me we will be here a long time! It seems to me you will be staying with me tonight!"

We protested: we had to get into Malawi *tonight*. We couldn't afford any more delays. But the sun was beginning to set over the Zambezi. It was now 4:30 p.m., and even if we left right away, we had an hour and a half to make a long drive to a border that would be even more hostile than the police here. We had to be reasonable.

"Look," Patrick said. "I have space for you to pitch your tents. And I'll make you dinner! I'm out of crocodile, so it'll have to be chicken."

So we sighed and thanked him and said, "All right." Yes, it was another delay. But delays happen, especially on the Race. Especially in Mozambique. So learn to adapt quickly, appreciate what you have, go ahead and fantasize about eating fried chicken instead of a rotten egg.

Besides, it seemed our presence lifted Patrick's spirits as much as his lifted ours.

At about 4:45 p.m., we were all thanking Patrick, Conrad, and James for their continued generosity. They had given up the day to help us. They didn't know us. They didn't owe us anything. They didn't care that *we* were supposed to be the do-gooders. They just took care of us.

It was decided that as soon as the police returned our passports, we would go to Patrick's house for the cookout. James was sent ahead to get the grill going. Our leaders were on the phone with Jarvis, who was still waiting for us at the border, even though we were now seven hours late. We told him that we wouldn't get to Malawi tonight, and apologized for our delay.

Meanwhile, Stacie and Michelle stormed into the station. We heard their voices all the way from outside. I couldn't tell what they were saying, but from what I was told later, it was along the lines of this:

"We are servants of God, and you are holding us up. You have to let us go. You have no reason to keep us here and keep up from doing the work of God. Do you want to be responsible for stopping what God is doing?"

I guess they didn't, because after 15 minutes, Stacie and Michelle sauntered out of the office with our 19 passports!

We cheered and I think Stacie said something like, "You can't hold up God, you just can't."

In the midst of our celebration and anticipation of one more night in Mozambique, Patrick and Conrad and the leaders had been talking. Phone calls were made. Opinions were sought. Plans were reconsidered. And at 5:05 p.m., a brash decision was made: in 55 minutes, over 30 miles, we were going to go for it.

In a frenzy, we gathered our water bottles and thanked Patrick as he shooed us back into the truck. We thanked him for his friendship and gave him Jaco's contact information, because he wanted to know more about this Jesus we were following who supposedly loved him despite his being a baddie.

We phoned Jarvis again and said we were going to try to come tonight after all. Jarvis said he would turn his car around and be there for us in Malawi.

We drove down the road a little way and stopped. It was 5:10. James, who had gone from grill master to chauffeur again, needed to get money from Patrick's house.

"We have money!" said Arden. "We don't need to stop!"

Patrick appeared to us one last time through the cage to laugh off our frantic offer: "We have money too!"

That was the last we saw of Patrick.

We were off. For real.

For the first time, the World Race became a race.

Whose idea was this? What made us think this was worth a try? We had a bumpy dirt road that our loaded truck would not maneuver well. It was getting dark. The border closed at 6:00 p.m. Even if we somehow made it to the border before then, we stood a slim chance of getting approved easily. But we'd need more time, because Malawi's border also closed at 6:00 and in between the two checkpoints was another five kilometer drive through no man's land. So if Mozambique let us out but we didn't get to Malawi in time, we could be illegally spending the night on a mountain road in our tents. If Mozambique didn't let us through, we would return to Patrick's in the dark and have that chicken dinner before attempting the same stunt tomorrow.

I felt detached from the crocodile truck. I watched us bounce in the dust, blinking with astonishment and exhaustion, the pink light of the sunset on the crowns of our heads, and it was like watching the climax of a movie. What a last-ditch effort we were making. Nothing was on our side. Failure was certain. We didn't know what we were doing. But we were going for it anyway. I wasn't scared or happy anymore. I was fascinated.

We drove as fast as possible but it wasn't fast enough. I kept staring straight ahead. So interested in what would happen.

At 5:30, the truck stopped in the middle of the road. It was dusk. The vehicle had overheated and James ran to fetch water. There were children all around us who had gathered to say hello but we couldn't see them since it was dusk and we were in that cage.

I yelled to ask James how much longer it would be to the border. "Not far."

It was 5:45. We moved again. The sky was completely black now. I couldn't see the stars or our headlights, but I could see the orange glow of cooking fires lining either side of the road like a heavenly race track.

At 5:50 we were praying and singing worship songs.

Then we were just quiet.

It was 6:00 and the border was closing.

It was 6:10 and we kept driving.

It was 6:20 and we kept driving.

Then, Arden saw a text message on his phone.

"Someone's at the border waiting for us!"

The text said to call Rupert and Ruth, whom we'd left back on the other side of the river. But all our cell phones were out of minutes so we couldn't call or text anyone.

At 7:00 p.m., we were there.

It was night. It was dark. The border was closed. The concrete offices were locked. Lonely street lights glowed in the distance. There were no cars or bikes or people.

The truck stopped and we shined phone lights out of the truck, trying to get our bearings. The lights landed on the silhouette of a tall man. He was approaching us.

Some of you we will not see before we go to heaven, but hopefully, some of you, we will see again soon...

More like "all of you."

"Jaco!"

"It's Jaco!"

"Rupert came!"

If I remember correctly, when Rupert and Ruth said goodbye to us before the bridge, they had started heading home to Gorongosa. But a couple hours later, when we were waiting at the police station with Patrick and company, someone had called them with the last of the cell phone minutes to ask for advice on what to do to reach the border in time. This made Rupert and Ruth turned the car around and tore through the bush themselves, trying to beat us to the border and smooth things out ahead of us.

"If you saw the way I drove," Rupert said, "you would have jumped out! I drove like a madman. Ruth didn't like it very much."

They found a different ferry, far upriver, and drove as fast as they could to tell border patrol that 19 Americans would be coming at closing time, and they had to stay open for us. When 6:00 came, the officials went home, but Rupert refused to leave. His presence forced one or two workers to stay there too. And when we finally arrived at 7:00, he requested the chief official to return and approve us to exit the country, or else they'd have a band of foreigners to deal with as well as this feisty South African couple.

The chief must have come, because our passports were soon collected.

We stood in the dark night, waiting. It was a little chilly. We called Jarvis on Ruth's phone, and Jarvis said that he was holding the Malawian border open on the other side. If we could get out of Mozambique, we could get into Malawi.

We were hungry. One of the teams had a thing of tuna salad that had been adventuring with us all day, so Oak found some crackers and rationed out a light dinner. We huddled together, smelling like tuna and grime and laughing at nothing and reassuring each other. We were too tired to know how we felt about all this. I think it had been such a day, the most we could do was to keep going, and keep waiting. We wouldn't feel relief until we were out of the country.

One thing we did feel, however, was tearful thankfulness for Rupert and Ruth, who had done so much more than they were obligated to, to try to get us out, and for Jarvis, who had been faithfully waiting at the Malawian border for 12 hours now, believing despite everything we would meet that night, and for James, Conrad, and Patrick, who had surrendered their truck, their money, and their day on a whim to help a squad of foreign strangers.

It had been nearly an hour without our passports and we were getting nervous. Would Malawi's border still be open if we exited Mozambique? Did they need a bribe here? Would they find any faults with our paperwork?

As I wondered these things, an official returned.

With 19 passports.

I opened my passport, and in it was a crisp, black, crooked exit stamp.

At 8:00 we climbed into the crocodile truck one last time and exited Mozambique. James drove us five kilometers through a mountain pass. We drove on dry, level ground with walls of rock on our right and left, and there was the promised Malawian border, glowing with hospitality and yellow lights.

The officials were all there. They smiled and said, "Welcome to Malawi." They weren't angry. They didn't interrogate us. Jarvis was there, welcoming us back and brushing off apologies for making him wait all day. The whole country might as well have stayed up late to welcome us in. That's how grand it was.

Rupert and Ruth had followed us to Malawi's border because Ruth had been needing to enter a different country for her Mozambican visa to remain valid anyway. So now, they were kicked out of Mozambique for seven days and had no choice but to drive with us to Blantyre. We all felt bad that they couldn't even go home.

"But missions is never easy," Rupert told us. "You've seen that today especially. It's all right. It's all part of it."

When we were all approved and packed in at 9:00 p.m. We thought it would all be downhill from there, but we had to drive uphill. Jarvis now had to drive us five hours to his mother's house in Blantyre, where we had been only three weeks ago when Mozambique wouldn't let us in.

Nine of us squeezed into the trunk of his van. It was a long, long ride. We sat on the floor with our knees up to our chins. Those who occupied the seats were even more crowded. Someone played an episode of *Downton Abbey* on a laptop and no one watched it. It was dark. We were sweaty and tired and grumpy and cramped. But we were in Malawi.

Jarvis drove the van up into the mountains on a twisting dirt road. Jarvis said that sometimes, people block the road with boulders and then rob travelers when they try to maneuver around them.

We didn't know it, because Jarvis didn't want to scare us, but we learned later that as we drove into the mountains, the gas light went on. We were alone in the middle of the night, miles from towns, and the van had to lug 19 people up a rocky road.

Jarvis stayed quiet, prayed, and gunned it. He prayed for the gas to last a little bit longer, a little bit longer, and it lasted two hours.

It lasted all the way through the mountains.

It lasted until we rolled into Blantyre. All of us were empty.

At 2:07 a.m. we were there. We fell out of the van and went into Jarvis' mother's house. The other half of C Squad was there. They had been there all August. They hugged us and gave us peanut butter and jelly sandwiches. We fell asleep on the floor.

We woke up silly.

We drove to ShopRite to buy snacks for the trip to Lake Malawi. It was a half hour before ShopRite opened, but we had just gone through two closed borders, so we pressed our noses on the windows and nodded to the employees and they shook their heads at us until 8:00, when the doors opened and we tore down the aisles, grabbing doughnuts and sodas and chips.

We boarded minibuses and took a five hour ride to Cape Maclear, on the shores of Lake Malawi. And now we have five days to rest and prepare for Asia.

On the Race, I have come to question God's promise to us: "I am with you." I've come to wonder if that's good enough for me. I don't want God to be with me; I want God to make everything good all the time. I have just been through three months of horrific travel, a death back home, and difficult ministry. Yet somehow, this climactic, miraculous, shitshow of an exodus answered my doubts.

The way out of Mozambique was bad and uncomfortable and exhausting, but it was *good*. It was unspeakably good. Because God was with us. When everything went wrong and there was no hope of efficiency or safety or fun, God was with us. God put us where He wanted us. God's presence turned a travel day into an awesome, redemptive miracle, worthy of books and tattoos. Rare is the day I believe in and witness the power of God with every bone and brain cell.

August 29
Cape Maclear, Malawi

The Parent Vision Trip is next. Those of us with parents visiting—10 out of 41 of us—will meet them in Chiang Mai. After they leave, the guys will go and the girls will stay and it'll be Manistry Month, when the men and women get to just be together. So I'll lose Oak and be on an all-girl team next month.

It was a good day! Arden dyed his beard purple and I dyed my hair purple. Kelsey cut her dreads off in Europe because she had lice in El Salvador, and she put a dread in each of the guys' sleeping bags months ago as a joke. Tony kept his all this time, and is now bragging to the squad that he just traded it for some jewelry from an artist by passing it off as "a real hair bracelet."

August 30
Cape Maclear, Malawi

Tomorrow we leave Africa.

Nate gave the safety briefing for Thailand. He's the safety point person for C Squad and his job is just to read the information about security the Georgia people give him. It's clearly a formality and he doesn't take it seriously. I find it funny when, every month, he says, "Okay, so, this next country is basically the same as the last one. Watch out for pickpockets and travel in groups."

I guess someone gave him feedback about it and told him to take it more seriously, so now he just doesn't preface the briefings with, "This country is the same as the last one."

I don't want to go on a bus ride, two planes, and another bus ride in the next couple days. I don't want to lose my team either. I'm also afraid of accidents, still. But if I think about that exodus for even a minute, every other little thing fades out. I can't get over how good God is. I am full of joy.

COUNTRY 9:
THAILAND

In which I see my parents,

sing to strangers, and

get sick of Christian music.

August 31
Flying from Lilongwe, Malawi to Nairobi, Kenya
I've always wanted to drop off the face of the earth. For the last three months, it feels like I have. With the spotty internet, different constellations, opposite seasons, and complete absence of schedule, our existence has just been something else.

But the next three months, I assume we will have technology and cities. We'll be on the map again.

September 1
The Bus from Bangkok to Chiang Mai, Thailand
Hot night. Humid night. Tired, but we all have our own seats! And we all get little bags with towelettes and coffee packets! And there's a separate compartment for our luggage!

September 2
Chiang Mai, Thailand
We're staying at a hostel and cafe that employs women who want to get away from working in the bars. The hostel has lots of murals and it's very clean. We don't have air conditioning in our rooms but there are fans and the windows open and the bunk beds are big and there's WiFi.

The showers are on the roofs. I've been taking cold showers but someone just pointed out that if I take a hot shower, the hottest I can stand, I'll feel cool instead of warm when I step back into the heat.

Mom and Dad will be here soon for the Parent Vision Trip. I'm excited and nervous.

It was sad to leave to Mom and Dad in January, but seeing them today was nothing but joy. All the parents arrived at the hostel, and we Racers ran downstairs to meet them.

I saw Mom first. She was wearing a bright blue shirt and had her iPhone trained on me. I waved and smiled and hopped the last few steps and ran into Dad first. I don't think we said anything, we just hugged a long time, grinning. Then Mom gave Dad the phone and she hugged me for even longer. She put her hands on my shoulders and looked at my face.

"You look the same. I love it," said Mom.

"Yeah!" I squealed dumbly. I tried not to cry but I did.

Reunions are the best damn things. All day, we've just been talking and talking and talking. We went to the night market and ate at an Irish pub. We laughed at each other. I told them about getting out of Mozambique. There are activities and worship sessions and service projects planned, but I just want to *talk* with them.

September 5
Chiang Mai, Thailand

Mom and Dad and Heidi and I went out to dinner, and we found a boutique hotel and ate in its restaurant. There weren't many people there. Only one other table was occupied, also by tourists.

Two musicians were performing, a girl named BiBi and a guy whose name I didn't get. BiBi sang pop covers and had eyeliner like Amy Winehouse and a perfect voice.

We were eating our big plates of mediocre food, and BiBi asked if anyone wanted to come up and sing a song.

"You should go up, Chels!" said Dad.

"Nah, I'm good."

We kept eating and BiBi sang another song and invited anyone again.

"Come on!" insisted Dad.

"Nooo."

"Sing *ADELE!*" he said, loud enough that BiBi heard him in that empty restaurant and saw me shaking my head. She asked, into the microphone, "Will you come up?"

I went up.

I didn't know many Adele songs, but I'd heard the chorus to "Rolling in the Deep," and it was in BiBi's binder. So I selected that, and began timidly butchering the first verse. After that, we moved on to "Someone Like You." I sat on a metal chair, pigeon-toed and hunched, wearing a pained grin, baggy elephant-print shorts, a baggy tank top, and a side ponytail.

Mom, Dad, and Heidi were *delighted*. The waitstaff came out and watched. I smiled and winced whenever I strained for high notes, as if to say, "I know, and I'm sorry."

September 7
Chiang Mai, Thailand

Mom and Dad left today. I'm sad to see them go and happy to be back with my friends.

Dad said the highlights of the trip were eating banana roti, visiting the slum, and seeing the girls' home in the mountains... but his favorite part of the entire trip was when I sang Adele songs in the restaurant.

I wanted to ask him and Mom, "Was I actually *that* good?" but they would have answered "yes" regardless, so I didn't.

But that's beautiful: it doesn't matter how *well* you can do things. God likes seeing you be brave and silly and try things out, period. It touches my heart that of all the incredible things on this trip, Dad really just liked it when I sang pop songs I didn't know to an empty room.

September 8
Chiang Mai, Thailand

I confessed to my team that I didn't feel dysfunctional enough with Mom and Dad.

All the people who had their parents visit seemed to have all this childhood baggage to confront, and they fought and wept and had breakthroughs. But me, I just had fun with Mom and Dad for a few days in Thailand.

But the whole team told me that it's great to have a healthy relationship. They could tell by looking at us that we were close and had a good time together.

Now that the parents have left, we are really focusing on our ministry: fighting sex trafficking by night and buying makeup at 7-11 by day.

We do most of our work at night in the red light district. Half of us go out to the bars and talk to the girls there and buy a little of their time and play Connect Four. "They *will* beat you at Connect Four," our host warned us. If they want, we pray for them and get their names to people who can try to get them get out if they indicate interest.

The other half of us stay back. We turn on worship music and pray for hours, and this activity lights up my cynicism.

We pray for the girls in the bars, that the injustice and violence they have seen would be defeated and redeemed. I know those are good things to pray, but my thighs stick to the couch and we pray for Jesus to come to Thailand like He wasn't there until we showed up and suggested it... and it's not working for me. I don't want to pray. Why? Am I a heretic, an asshole, or a burnout?

God, I know you love us. You want us to know you. You show up. You put us where you want us. These are things I know for sure. What I do not know for sure is why we pray the same things and play the same songs with the same words and the same four chords.

Here's the entire stunted vocabulary of worship music: Jesus, love, heart, river, you, closer, surrender, mountain, wreck, deep, wash, sin, Lord, power, name, way, rescue, pull, push, yeah, oh, ah, ooh, yeah. This feeble attempt to articulate and celebrate divine truth erodes my faith.

I want to go see what's outside instead. I want to wander around and see the Buddhist temples right now, which are like cathedrals if cathedrals were gold and red and redolent of sweet incense. They have ribbons and bells and gongs. I want to be *there*.

I think of the nine countries I've seen this year, and what God has done in them, and the people I've met, and the troubles and the joys, and I soak in the power of God's presence. But at the same time, I'm *tired* of World Race spirituality, and no one else seems to be. It makes me feel separated from my teammates.

At a nearby temple, there's a thing called Monk Chat, where tourists can go talk with monks and learn about their lives and Buddhist traditions. We are supposed to do that as a sort of supplemental "ministry."

I love Monk Chat but I'm not really doing it as ministry. I'm doing it as a way to learn. That's the right thing to do, I think. If we treat it as ministry, if we go with a heart to teach but not to learn, then how can anything meaningful come up? No, I don't want to convert the monks. I want to be converted by them a little. Is there not room in the life of a Christian to listen to the people we are sent to? What if they have something we need to hear?

September 9
Chiang Mai, Thailand
Thailand is unique in that lots of families knowingly send their children "to the city" to work in the sex trade and support them. They aren't being tricked into thinking there are real jobs there. They know.

It's creepy to walk through the red light district, past a hundred bars, beckoned in by 14-year-old girls who say they're 18. It's creepy to see expats and business travelers that look so normal—usually white, usually men, with normal smiles and good manners and familiar brand name clothing—frequenting these bars night after night. It's evil. The evil is eerily subtle when the men act cheerful and polite in the bars. It's blatant when your teammates return, shaken, from visiting a restaurant where you can order people off a menu.

If God took us out of Mozambique, God can get these people out too, who are in a flawed system that leads into sex work and with whom we play Connect Four and feel helpless. The system is against them, but that won't stop Jesus. The system was against us in Mozambique and He led *us* out.

Maybe that exodus from Mozambique is profound for that reason: I've never been at odds with the powerful people. I've always had the regime on my side. I'm white and American and rich. If I fall on hard times, I can fall back on my family and money and education.

What about the people who can't trust those structures?

And in what ways have I been on the side of the empire, the oppressors? Missionaries can be without even thinking about it, without intending to. It's so easy to do. It's built into the history of missions.

I'm a World Racer. I want to be sent by God to love the world. I can't do that well if I don't understand where *I* come from. I wish my squad talked about this more. Maybe it doesn't *occur* to us to really look at our situations back home. Relative to most of the world, we are so wealthy that we can go traveling for a year, coasting on savings and our rich friends' generosity. Maybe the implications of questioning our motives for going on missions are potentially too sinister.

But I cannot write off missions. I've met so many missionaries this year who have been nothing but forces of holiness and love and respect. Their words are true, kind, and necessary. They indicate that there is *something* good, true, and beautiful here.

And I still do believe I was *called* to this trip. I was not called to teach English in Turkey or be a beach bum in Southeast Asia. I was called *here*.

I think it's complicated.

But it hinges on the person of Jesus, doesn't it? God, the omnipotent, omnipresent Source of Being, squeezed into a sack of skin and pitched His tent among us and chose to be a member of a group against whom the system was stacked. So God is with us, and I don't mean "God's thinking about you from the clouds" or whatever, I mean that God actually became one of us and was literally killed... there's such a mashup of power and weakness in the Incarnation. It is worth wrestling with.

September 11
Chiang Mai, Thailand

We talked to one monk at Monk Chat who actually grew up in a Christian home and converted to Buddhism. I haven't met any Thai people with that story yet.

The monk seemed unsatisfied with his life. I asked him what his favorite story about the Buddha was, and he said, "I don't know. I'm not interested. I know more about Jesus."

You're not making my intention to embrace Buddhist ideas very easy, buddy, I thought with a smirk.

"Do you think you'll become a Christian again?" I asked.

"I don't know," he replied. "I think I want to make money."

I haven't been able to work out much this year, and I eat what they give me and supplement it with Coke, but I don't know if I've ever loved my body as much as I do now. My hair is starting to fall out more, probably from not getting enough protein, and I'm always sweating, and I'm bitten and *still* not tan, but being in this body that's brought me around the world in sickness and health inspires nothing but thankfulness.

September 12
Chiang Mai, Thailand

Intercession time again. A little bit ago, I told my team how my piety's getting ragged, how I'm sick of the lingo and the Hillsong albums, how I'm questioning mission work...

I was afraid of this all-women team being high-maintenance, but *I* feel like the high-maintenance one. I'm always getting disillusioned with this, problematizing that. There I go again; I can't fall into the love of God and be a light to the nations like everyone else.

Anyway, I had my little rant to the team and was afraid I'd get constructive feedback on it. But no one was upset with me. Stephanie and Tara said they have those questions too.

When I get in my head like this, I forget that I'm not alone. I forget how freeing it is to just say what's going on in my head. I write too much. It never occurs to me to talk.

September 16
Chiang Mai, Thailand
Stephanie said that my blog about getting out of Mozambique was incredible.

I think I'm going to keep writing once the Race is over.

Tomorrow, we're going to go out and play worship music on the street corner and pray for people. I'm in such a funk about it. I'm so sick of going up to strangers and asking to pray for them. I'm so sick of hearing the music. I don't want to perform it. I don't want to go. It's going to be stupid and creepy and I don't want to.

September 17
Chiang Mai, Thailand
My team decided to go to the night market, play some songs, and hold up signs saying "Free Prayer."

I did not want to.

I didn't want to practice songs on my mandolin because the mandolin is hard. I didn't want to play worship music because I'm tired of hearing it all the time. I didn't want to have signs saying "Free Prayer," because people would just laugh at us and be creeped out. I didn't want to go out because I was tired.

I said I didn't feel like doing it, and my team said I didn't have to and I felt like an ass. They said if I wanted to pray or do something else, that was fine. So I stared at the floor for a long time and said I'd just do it, because I felt obligated to cowboy up.

At 8:00 we went and sat on the steps to the mall with my mandolin, Stephanie's guitar, and Tara's ukulele, and we played our set, which was two songs: "This Little Light of Mine" and "Lean on Me." It took four minutes.

Then we tried to play other songs by memory: worship music, Adele, Katy Perry. We sang songs we learned in Africa. We banged on stuff and sang "When I'm Gone" like Anna Kendrick in *Pitch Perfect*.

It was awkward and a little unpleasant. Jinnae and Courtney held up the "Free Prayer" signs and no one asked to be prayed for. Tara took her straw hat and set it in front of us. "Put a few coins in!" she said. "Let's see if we make money."

A Chinese couple approached. The woman broke into a grin. She stared while her husband took a picture with a big camera. She sat down next to Jinnae and posed for a picture. She motioned to us to keep singing and her husband took a video. She put money in the hat. I do not know why she was so happy.

A man came and asked us for a song and we played "Lean on Me" again. He stood and listened to the whole thing and put money in the hat and thanked us. We made 60 baht, which is about two dollars, enough to buy three plain roti, or two with Nutella.

We had been at it for an hour and a half and were putting away our instruments when a boy in an orange safety vest rode up on his bike. The bike was decorated with duct tape, and a Hot Wheels box was tied down on the back of it. The boy—let's call him D—had a stack of papers with a picture of him and something written in Thai. He handed one to us, and we asked what it said. He didn't answer. Instead, he elbowed his way into the middle of our group and motioned for Tara's ukulele. He strummed it and gave it back and asked for Stephanie's guitar, which he flipped over and started drumming on. He started singing, and stopped when we didn't join him. We couldn't figure out what he was saying, until we heard the familiar chorus.

"Oh! It's 'Have You Ever Seen the Rain?' we exclaimed, and started singing along. But then D stopped us and indicated we were to start from the beginning. We didn't know the words to the verse, so we sang, "Na, na, na, na, na, na, na, I know! Blah, blah, na, na, na, na… I wanna know, have you ever seen the rain?"

He had us sing several songs. Then he took a break to demonstrate a dizzying mastery of English profanity and strum the guitar too hard, and he flipped it back over and laid down another beat. Then he sang a few solos, and all the while, people stopped to photograph us.

"Today," said D, "is happy birthday for me! I am thirteen!"

We cheered for him and sang "Happy Birthday." Then D sang it again. And again.

After a half hour or so, D decided it was time to go, and said good night. We gave him our earnings for the evening and told him to have a happy birthday, even though we doubted it really was his birthday.

I have always admired people like that. I don't even mean the big things like living in a van or walking across America or proposing to your girlfriend with a flash mob. I mean things like talking to strangers, and singing on the street corner. Instead of saying, "Wouldn't it be funny if…?" they do the funny things. Or the stupid things. Or the hard things. Or the awkward things. Or the loving things. Those people are my heroes.

Tonight wasn't the most fun or memorable night of the Race. But it was better than I expected. I set aside my pride and chose to get a little awkward, and God elevated my clumsy, half-assed actions to something better. Tourists got excited. Passersby got a laugh. A kid got a present, and who cares if it was his birthday or not.

September 22
Chiang Mai, Thailand
Conrad, Patrick's friend, from the Mozambique exit, with the crocodile truck… *died.*

Of malaria.

We just heard.

He'd been in Mozambique, what, 20 years? And we met him less than a month before the end.

Some people are in touch with Patrick on Facebook. He said he's not drunk as much these days.

September 27
Chiang Mai, Thailand

The squad is back together in Chiang Mai and we're about to get put on new teams. We are in the middle of another worship set at another debrief. Another ten minutes of singing "Your Presence."

There are few moments like this left, but not so few that I cherish them.

I hope God puts me on Tony's team. I was so excited about being placed on his team at training camp and then it didn't happen, and we haven't spent much time together this year. I know God doesn't have to, but I just want to file that request.

September 28
Chiang Mai, Thailand

We were put on new teams and guess what? I'm on a team with Tony! And Arden, Kori, Belle, Robyn, and Bre. Our ministry this month in Cambodia is teaching in a seminary.

When I found out, my knees buckled and I actually screamed in joy! I have never in my life actually buckled, I'm not sure I even believed that was a real thing. I was immediately embarrassed. But I'm so happy to be with my favorite people, and we are going to a college and I'll finally do ministry I'm good at: teaching and being intellectual.

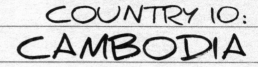

COUNTRY 10:
CAMBODIA

In which I become a professor,

eat a snake off a skewer,

and think about a boy.

10

11

12

September 29
Phnom Penh, Cambodia

The bus left Chiang Mai last night at 7:00 p.m. Each seat had its own cartoonish fleece blanket and up front were fake flowers in plastic vases.

The air vents on the right side of the bus leaked. We tried to go to sleep, but cold water dripped all over us. We stuffed the blankets into the vents, but that just made the leaks worse elsewhere. So we all squished onto the left side of the bus.

We were at the border in the morning. It reminded me of Africa: dusty, noisy, three-hour wait, lots of paperwork.

A different bus was waiting for us on the Cambodia side. The seats were squishy and there were chintzy curtains in the windows, with fringe. I called them chintzy and Tony nodded.

"I agree. They're very nice," he said.

"No, they're *chintzy*. I mean they're tacky," I said.

"'Chintzy' means fancy. It's a good thing," he said.

"No, 'chintzy' means tacky and cheap."

"No, it means nice."

I knew I was correct but I let it drop.

The ride was supposed to be six hours but it was closer to nine. No one cares about stuff like that anymore.

It was too bright and hot on the bus to open the curtains much, but when I peeked outside, I saw bright green rice paddies and tall skinny trees, and it occurred me that we were in *Cambodia*.

It's become old to be in a new country. When we landed in Honduras and took what I thought was a long—90-minute—drive to the village of La Ermita, I was captivated by the rolling hills and the colorful, shabby houses that covered them for miles and miles. We were in a new place! We didn't know what to expect at all! It was exciting because wherever we were, we were *not* in America.

Now, we are in another new country. Our *tenth* new country. We don't know the people we're working with this month. We don't know what we'll eat or if we'll have air conditioning. We don't know Khmer. I think for many, that much uncertainty would be worrying.

But one priceless gift this year has given me is the capacity not to fret. It's come through nine months of fretting, but I seem to be getting the hang of it now. I am content when I don't have control over the travel. I can be content when I go home and realize that I still don't have control over my life... and God is *still* good. How freeing, to rejoice in the wildness and uncertainty of my existence, rather than tamping down our neuroses with coping mechanisms and rigid routines.

When I get home in about two months, I want to bring this back with me: I want to see my life, whatever happens, as the adventure it really is. I want to find strange things in the familiar, and familiar things in the strange. The Race helps me live that way because I know ahead of time that I'm "traveling around the world to eleven countries in eleven months." But since normal life isn't forecasted in monthly chunks, it's going to be easy to feel forever stuck in the doldrums instead of on a grand journey which does, at times, require periods of waiting and drifting. I hope I do well when it is time to return.

Anyway, after almost a solid day of bus, bus, bus, potty break, border, bus, bus, bus, we were eventually deposited on a dark, dank corner quite late at night in Phnom Penh, and slumped there for a while until tuk tuks, open-air auto rickshaws, took us on a ride.

There are few physical sensations more delightful than going fast on a tuk tuk on a warm night in a new city.

Now, I'm sitting in clean furniture in the lobby of a hostel. Norah Jones is playing and there's air conditioning. It is one of those times everything feels easy and I say all that nice stuff about adventure and remark, "I just *love* international travel."

Tomorrow we go to the seminary.

September 30

A seminary on the outskirts of Phnom Penh, Cambodia

This seminary is big and airy. We are staying on the top floor, a loft with a big common area and bedrooms with space for Michelle, Robyn, and Kori. I volunteered to sleep on a low bed outside the room on a thin mattress. My mattress has Tom and Jerry on it, and, in size 72 Times New Roman font, "I want to make you happy because seeting you smilig makes me happy."

On the floor below us, there's a sanctuary, kitchen, school offices, bathrooms, and a cavernous multi-purpose space. There's a balcony on either side: on the left, you can see a shipping yard and on the right, a flooded field with cows and an old bathtub floating in it. And the floors below are dorms and classrooms.

Very happy. Love my team, which is named Twelve, because the 11 months of the Race are coming to an end.

October 1

Phnom Penh, Cambodia

Our host is Pastor Timothy. He has a quiet, kind demeanor. He's never hosted Racers before. He's full of energy and tells us about the amazing things he's seen at this school. Like, there's a pond outside where students take walks, and a while ago, the water was getting dirty, so Timothy prayed about it and then flowers appeared and filtered the water and now the pond is clean and lily pads float on its surface.

Timothy asked Team Twelve what our areas of expertise were. I said I knew writing, English, music, geography, and world religions, so he said, "Please teach us those things."

There hasn't been a month of the Race where ministry had been tailored to my qualifications. It's nice. In the morning I taught English for the first time with Bre. In the afternoon I taught geography with Tony.

But I'm nervous to teach writing, and I'm scared to teach world religions, because what if I don't know enough, or if I offend them by being too sympathetic to other traditions?

I feel inferior to the students here because a lot of them are older than me and most of them are men. I know it shouldn't make a difference, but I'm afraid they won't take me seriously because I'm a woman. *I'm* not in grad school. Who am I to teach them?

But I am *deliriously* happy to be with Tony. We had fun teaching geography together today. I haven't seen him this often since El Salvador, and I swear he's mellowed and grown more caring. He's just wonderful.

October 3
Phnom Penh, Cambodia

I woke up at 5:30 a.m. today and stumbled down to the chapel for devotions.

We stood for the first hymn, and then Timothy had us sit down, and then we sang the second hymn, which was called "Stand Up, Stand Up For Jesus." Tony and I exchanged mirthful glances and have been laughing about it all day.

October 6
Phnom Penh, Cambodia

For dinner, Timothy took Twelve to a Chinese restaurant. We sat around a big table and ate duck and stuff. Timothy told us to go to Banff when we returned to America, except he said "Bampoo."

"I met a man from Germany who said it was *more beautiful* than Switzerland."

"In Canada?" said Kori.

"Yeah."

"Wow."

"You *should* go there. I think that's the best."

"Banff?"

"Bampoo."

"Bampoo?"

"Bampoo."

October 7
Phnom Penh, Cambodia

For dinner we had just bread and potatoes. We were out of everything else.

October 9
Phnom Penh, Cambodia

Last week, I went to meet my writing students and found that I had been paired with a group of four men, each of whom is pursuing a master's degree and is older than me. No one had brought papers to work on. They just asked me what I had planned for our "class."

I told them I didn't know, and I didn't know what to expect. I was flustered. It was the feeling we'd get at churches in Africa when the pastor looked at our team and said, "Who will be preaching today?" Except this time, I was alone. These guys had been in seminary for years. What did I have to teach *them*?

They asked me what I could teach. I told them I could help with writing and English. They asked what else I could teach. So I told them I knew about world religions and music and Latin and Greek. I wanted them to be interested in languages, but they weren't. Their ears perked up when I mentioned religions. While I smiled dumbly, my guys planned what they wanted to learn: all the world religions. Also, singing and music.

I raced upstairs to our room afterwards in a panic and started going through my computer, scouring old folders for notes from college. I'd just agreed to lecture for an hour every day on a different religion, and I was *not* ready. Did I know enough to fill an hour? What if they had questions I didn't have answers to? What if I said inaccurate things? What if they were bored? What if they already knew everything I'd tell them? What if they didn't respect me as a woman and a younger person than them?

All this hovered overhead as I wrote lists of things I knew about Judaism. I wrote down the things that interested me. I wrote down dates and names. I wrote down ways it's not the same as Christianity.

The next day, I started lecturing on the basics of Jewish belief and culture and was surprised to find that my fears had been unnecessary: the guys *were* interested. I knew more than I thought. A lot more. I had answers to a lot of questions, and the ones I didn't know just led to good discussions. I was plenty qualified. It was fun to teach about something I cared about. I liked connecting my knowledge with what they already knew. I liked teaching them new terms. I liked sharing why it mattered to study other religions.

The hour passed too quickly and I offered to take another day looking at some topics in Judaism more closely, but they said they wanted to hear about another religion. So I felt intimidated again and raced upstairs again to start refreshing my understanding of Islam.

The next day, the same thing happened: I went in feeling scared and dumb, they talked, I talked, we all enjoyed ourselves, and they called for another religion, so I raced upstairs and began the hours of studying and organizing information all over again.

It's a lot of work, doing all this research. When I have time between other classes, I study and prepare lectures and figure out how to best format the talks for students of Christian theology. It's hard work. It stretches my brain. It feels great.

October 10
Phnom Penh, Cambodia
I'm constipated.

October 13
Siem Reap, Cambodia
We drove to Siem Reap to see Angkor Wat! It took 10 hours to get here.

The place was amazing. It felt like a creepy theme park. We hired tuk tuks for the day and they drove us around to all the temple complexes. We paid a random person to be our tour guide. He wasn't an official one, but he knew a lot. We prayed for him at the end of our time and he was into it.

We walked around the whole day talking about the last time we all had hard ciders and resolved to look for some in the evening. When we came back we found a Hard Rock Cafe down the street from our hostel. With our $2.50 dinner budget, we planned to get something cheap to eat on the street, then go there for cider. But when we looked at the menu, with its burgers... we thought we'd split an entree. Then we decided we'd all order our own. Then we ordered more ciders. It was worth blowing the budget for.

We saw Lenny Kravitz's guitar, and watched a band perform. The woman who sang was probably six-foot-five and gorgeous and played a tambourine the whole time, and the guy singer had a shaved head except for a top knot and he danced like his life depended on it but sat on a tall stool the entire time.

The night bus back to Phnom Penh was cramped. It was hard to sleep on my plastic seat.

We stopped late at night at one of those night market truck stops and we, for probably the hundredth time this year, stumbled outside at that ungodly hour, looked at all the unfamiliar snacks, and bought the cheapest ones. We used the toilets, which were in a dark, creepy, concrete building. Our waste ran into a channel outside and I thought of the pig farm in Albania.

We sat on dirty plastic lawn furniture under the flickering orange lights, eating our stuff, sharing it with one another, and Arden looked around and up at the rafters and smiled the nicest smile.

"I'm really happy, you know?" he said. "This is a good moment. I'm really happy to be here."

It hadn't occurred to me to examine the moment, but as soon as he said that, even though I was a little grumpy and sleepy, I was happy too.

October 17
Phnom Penh, Cambodia
Tonight, Tony took the barbequed snake we bought on the riverbank by the palace and chased Kori and Robyn all around with it. The snake was coiled and skewered and it looked nasty after being out for hours.

Arden and I sat at the table watching, and he ate an orange and dropped the peel in a bowl of soy sauce left from dinner.

When I'm on the balcony at sunset and night, I see the small, flooded fields. I see the bathtub on its wooden pallet. Some of the shipping crates say "Evergreen." I hear airplanes taking off. I can see the tops of them speeding down what appears from the balcony to be the next street over but what is, of course, a runway. This bizarre landlocked harbor, where huts and floods and herds can be next door to an international airport. It's a liminal place.

October 18
Phnom Penh, Cambodia
In between classes, we're cataloguing the school library using the Library of Congress, as if we have any idea how to do that. I don't even know how to use "Library of Congress" in a sentence. The library is a room full of shelves with old books from mostly Presbyterian authors. Arden has built a big spreadsheet and we pick up each book and decide how to categorize it. We thought it would be straightforward: put the Bibles on that shelf, reference materials on that one, fiction here, systematic theology there… but it's hard.

I wrote a list before leaving for the Race of the things that scared me most about this trip. Seeing as I've been on the road for almost ten months, I thought it would be interesting to revisit that list and see what's happened with those fears.

I was afraid of getting shots.
This was the biggest, scariest challenge I faced as I prepared for the Race. In order to even decide to apply, I had to come to terms with the fact that I'd need to go to a travel doctor. After going through with it, I'll say that while shots still freak me out more than they should, I'm no longer crippled by that fear. All those shots didn't stop me from doing the Race, and I know that they can't stop me from doing other things in the future.

I was nervous about meeting my fundraising deadlines.
I met every single fundraising deadline and was fully funded with time to spare, thanks to you all.

I was scared of long, claustrophobic bus and plane rides.
I was right to be. I am now surprised when a bus I'm on reaches its destination on time… or at all. Travel has been hard. But we've done it. And we haven't been in a single accident, even a minor one! My horrific travel day stories are some of my favorites from this year.

I was afraid of not being able to sleep on those long, claustrophobic journeys.
I can't sleep on those journeys, no. But it doesn't scare me anymore. I've learned two things. One: if I don't get a good night's sleep, it's no fun, but it's not the end of the world. I'll be fine. Two: the aisle on buses is a bumpy place to spend the night, but I can at least be horizontal.

I was afraid of hot weather.
C Squad has had a mild route compared to many Racers. Aside from Southeast Asia, which I knew would be a different story, only El Salvador has been unbearably hot. We were in Europe in the spring and it was rainy and mild. We were in Southern Africa in the winter, which was equally pleasant. Southeast Asia is hot, but I got used to it. There are fans here, and a product called Prickly Heat Cooling

Powder, which I'm constantly making a mess with. But mostly, the way to deal with the heat is to stay hydrated, stop complaining, and embrace the new atmosphere like it's embracing me.

I was afraid to get sick.
I've been relatively healthy this year. Yes, I get strange digestive issues about once a month from eating weird things. Yes, I keep Imodium in my purse. But for the most part, I've been fine.

Getting sick is no fun, though. In Zambia I spent an entire day in our host's dark house, alone and nauseated, and it was scary and lonely and depressing. A week or so later, I was still sick and started feeling confused and exhausted, and I was afraid I'd let myself get dehydrated, or had contracted malaria. But an hour later, I was leaving the hospital with a prescription that cleared up everything right away. I actually have not thrown up on the Race once.

I was afraid to eat gross stuff.
In Zambia I ate two peanut butter and jelly sandwiches every day. I don't like peanut butter, but I eat it now. And I've eaten funny things. Our team just went downtown and on the banks of the Mekong River, we bought snake kabobs, crickets, a tarantula, and quail eggs. The tarantula was the worst because it tasted like a Gusher made of meat. The snake tasted like canned tuna.

I was afraid of losing my Nook.
I lost my Nook! I left it on my bed in El Salvador for the day, and when I returned, someone had snatched it through the window, along with my external hard drive and a bag of candy. It was devastating, but my wonderful parents were able to buy me another one and mail it to our coaches, who gave it to me at our Houston layover on the way to Europe. I do not leave my new Nook by windows anymore.

I was afraid of ticks.
I have had no tick problems.

I was afraid of getting bored with my clothes.
My clothes are always changing! We trade clothes with each other all the time. My wardrobe is almost completely different than it was in January.

I was afraid of team changes.
That happened. A lot. I was on Crisco (before the Race began), switched to Brazen Hearts for January to March, then to Deep Roots in April, then to Team Oak for May through August, then Skittles in September. Now I'm on Team Twelve—the revamped Crisco. Team changes are tough, but they happen and I'm used to them. And it's good if they're painful! It means I love my team.

I was afraid of something bad happening to my family back home.
Nothing bad has happened to my immediate family, but I am disturbed and grieved about the death I've encountered this year. In July my sister Kate's close friend passed away unexpectedly and it has scarred me and my community in Washington. Many people on our squad have experienced deaths back home too. It feels like one of those seasons. It is scary and sad and it reminds me that we're mortal.

I was afraid to miss my sister's high school graduation and my dad's 50th birthday.
I did and it was sad.

I was afraid of not making the most of the time given to me.
There have been times I haven't taken all my opportunities, and I regret some of those times. But it's been ten months: no one's perfect at that every day.

I was afraid of goodbyes.
It was hard to say goodbye to my family and friends when I left. Uprooting every month hasn't been as hard as I thought, because I haven't connected with every place in the same way. The final goodbyes in several weeks will be as hard as leaving my family, I expect.

I was afraid of forgetting about Jesus and turning the World Race into some sort of self-help expedition.
Yeah. World Racers aren't automatically spiritually healthy because we're on a mission trip, and prioritizing our relationship with God can be just as challenging, nuanced, frustrating, and rewarding as it is at home. Being on the Race doesn't change our personalities or habits or vices either.

So.

Many of these fears have become non-issues and a couple have come true. But I like seeing the growth. Even though God says, "Fear not, for I am with you," I go and get scared of things anyway. But it's amazing to look back and see that when I face my fears, or am forced to face them, God shows up and brings me through.

October 20
Phnom Penh, Cambodia
Tony and I went to the store and on the way back I asked how he'd changed this year. He said it was a hard question because he just kind of absorbs feedback and experiences and updates the algorithms, or something like that. I was unsatisfied with that answer but then he asked me and I said it was hard to answer too and I'd have to check my journal, so I guess that was also unsatisfying. At least I didn't use the word "algorithm."

I've realized that I can't keep a straight face around Tony.

Kori and I lay side by side in her bed tonight. She and I have had so many fights and misunderstandings this year. I've never met someone I've had conflict with like that. I never know when to feel guilty and when to feel defensive.

But tonight I was lying next to her in her twin bed and we were talking about life after the Race. I told her that I wanted to act. I wanted to pursue theatre. I've been scared to tell people that but I told her. She was supportive. She asked if I was going to go back to school first, and I said no.

It was a tender thing, to be next to each other and say kind things about each other's dreams.

October 22
Phnom Penh, Cambodia

Tony entered the men's bathroom as I was heading to the women's. In the shower, I noticed the sound of his shower through the vent in the wall... and somehow this is worth mentioning.

October 23
Phnom Penh, Cambodia

This month, there has been a routine and it's been good, even though I pride myself on being go-with-the-flow. Last night, I didn't want to listen to a podcast or anything. I just wanted to pray a little. I felt at home in my head. Whenever I feel like that, I know I'm on the right track.

The chapel was empty this evening and I went in and played Khachaturian's Toccata. Tony said he loves Bach's Fugue in D Minor so I downloaded a copy and played that too.

He came into the chapel and sat in a chair far away from me, and I don't know if he was dozing off or listening to the music, but from across the room, I swear I felt electricity.

Leave It All

October 26
Phnom Penh, Cambodia
We leave tomorrow.

Last night was the first night I lost sleep thinking about Tony.

October 27
Back at the Envoy Hostel in Phnom Penh, Cambodia
Today's goodbye to the students was the first one of the Race that made me cry. All the students gathered and sang a song that they said meant "love forever." A few gave us beaded cross keychains. Pastor Timothy gave each of us a box of "the best Korean parasite medicine, to take when you're back home." We prayed together in the entryway.

Tomorrow, C Squad will fly to Kuala Lumpur, where we'll be working at a school. I can't believe we're going to our last country.

COUNTRY 11:
MALAYSIA

The month I get a staph infection,

finish the Race, and,

most importantly, kiss a boy.

October 28
Kuala Lumpur, Malaysia
We are at a Montessori school in a big mustard cement complex in a big ugly parking lot with a Catholic church across one street and a park across another and lots of convenience stores and Indian and Chinese restaurants every way we look.

The girls' room is too hot and it has one bunk bed too many and it is claustrophobic. Kori thinks she has another staph infection and is dehydrated but won't drink water, so now she has heartburn too. I don't feel sorry for her and she's annoying me. I'm trying. I brought her food, prayed, brought water, and switched beds so she could have the bottom bunk. Then I had to get out. It's just too crowded and hot in there. There is an air conditioning unit on the wall but we don't know if we're allowed to use it yet. Please, God!

Down the hall from our room are two showers and a small, dim sitting room with an ugly couch and blue walls and an old television and a larger common room adjacent. There are unfinished wooden shelves and more ugly furniture and one wall that is all windows. I'm sitting on a sofa against that wall now.

The guys are on the floor above us. They feel far away. I want to be there. I thought about Tony the whole flight here.

We have only three weeks left.

October 30
Kuala Lumpur, Malaysia
I don't get along with Kori, I'm infatuated with Tony, and I want to go home.

In today's argument, Kori told me I'm hard to get close to. It hurt my feelings, but I'm trying not to let it get to me. I'm not hard to get close to.

Right?

No one's ever told me that before but maybe that's because they don't get close enough to me to be able to even say that.

Leave It All

I'm scared that maybe I'm hard to get close to.

Okay, there's something with Tony. I feel the electricity constantly now.

He goes places with me. He's considerate. There are few people whose company I never tire of, and he is one of them. I can't get enough of him.

Like yesterday. I was helping with the school choir and I offered to play the cajón on a song, and he said later that he was worried for me because my skirt didn't pass my knees so maybe it would be tricky to straddle the drum and play. Who would notice that? A boy who cares about you and notices the length of your skirt, that's who.

But I don't *want* romance because I don't want anyone messing up my nonexistent life plans. Relationships are complicated. My greatest desire is to fall in love and share the rest of my life with another human... but not if it inconveniences me in literally any way.

A letter I won't deliver:

Dear Tony,

My computer's at three percent and I'd write more, but I don't have my charger. I'm guessing Arden's still using it, *and* that when he's done with it, you'll be the one running to our floor to return it to me. You're thoughtful like that.

I missed you in Honduras. I felt at home around you at Launch and at the airports, and then you weren't there. The Race was new and I was disoriented, and I knew that if you had been around, I would have felt at home. You are one of the most peaceful presences I know. I hope we can sit together on the plane home. It's a long shot, but hey. I don't care how long the flights or buses are if I'm near you.

It's easy for me to remember times with you. Watching *Garden State* in El Salvador. The first night I hugged you by way of greeting was in Tirana, at the top of the stairs at the hostel. Trying to watch *Arrested Development* over and over with bad internet. Last month, all those times you talked to me late into the night, or just hung out with me for no reason. The pancakes you made.

Two percent battery now, okay, listen, one more thing. Just let me say that I'm afraid I'll suck at this. I'm scared to hurt and be hurt. I'm scared we don't agree on big things. But I'm open because you are wonderful and I can't help but smile around you and your heart and mind inspire me and like I said, with you I'm at home.

October 31
Kuala Lumpur, Malaysia

Did library organizing again. Two months of cataloging in a row! I spent all day with Tony and didn't want it to end.

I'm so distracted. I don't want to be sidetracked from the other things God is doing this month. I don't want to take this epic journey only to wither into the throes of infatuation for a boy on the final month.

On Tuesday, we flew from Phnom Penh, Cambodia to Kuala Lumpur, Malaysia. It's hard to properly articulate how grateful I was for the two hour flight after months of two-day-long bus rides. It was amazing. I boarded a plane, watched an episode of *Mr. Bean*, and ate chicken lasagna. I wasn't even annoyed when the stranger in front of me reclined all the way into my lap. By the time I calculated that the drive to Kuala Lumpur would have taken 40 hours, we were landing in Malaysia.

Team Twelve met our hosts at the airport and we went to a cluster of tall buildings, one of which houses the Montessori school. The school occupies space in four others, providing education to nearly 1000 students of all ages.

Leave It All

This is the last week of school before the holiday, so my team won't work with many students. Instead, we'll be repainting classrooms, organizing a library, and doing other odd jobs. When I learned this, I was happy. I like organizing books, and I don't mind painting.

But God had a special treat.

When we left our seminary last month, I thought I had played a piano for the last time on the Race. But it turns out that the school choir has been aching for a live accompanist, and so this week, for four hours a day, I get to do something I'm good at. I can sight read the music and teach the singers their parts. I can turn my own pages and watch the conductor and transpose on the spot. It's like I haven't been away for 10 months. I'm accompanying a choir and I'm *good* at it.

For the majority of the Race, I haven't had a piano. In Guatemala, I had a pickaxe and someone told me to break up a boulder and build a road. In El Salvador, I had a classroom of preschoolers I couldn't stop from peeing their pants and hitting each other. In Albania I had a broom to dip in whitewash and paint pig stalls. In Malawi I had doors to knock on.

Most of the time on the Race, I don't get to control my job, and odds are I won't be great at it. I get a task and I'm just supposed to bless people, regardless of my expertise or enthusiasm. This has been challenging, and a major way I have come up short this year: most of the time, I haven't been passionate about the ministry, and I've slipped into doing the bare minimum, justifying my laziness by saying, "Well, I'm not *ultimately* called to missions."

But when I've invested anyway, God has done powerful work in me. I'm becoming someone who can work humbly and faithfully at pretty much anything. I'll always choose a piano over a pickaxe, but I'm learning to set aside my preferences for the sake of serving the people around me. So in these last three weeks of ministry on the Race, pray for my team and me to throw ourselves into all the ministry we can, whether we are experts or amateurs, whether we are tired or energetic, and whether we are happy to be here or anxious to go home.

November 2
Kuala Lumpur, Malaysia

Tony and I went to mass last night for All Saints Day. It was dimly lit for the Novena, whatever that is.

He forgot his wallet and asked if I had any money when the offering sacks approached. I had a 50 ringgit bill and some ones (three ringgit is about one dollar). I showed him my wallet and asked which he wanted to give.

"Pick one," he said. I looked at him and dropped the 50. They took an offering for the poor later and I put the ones in then. I plan not to accept all the 50 back from him. It can be from both of us.

Today, in front of the whole team, he said, "Chelsea, last night at mass, you demonstrated extreme generosity, and it wasn't forced or a matter of obligation, it was just instinctive." I didn't remember what he was referring to at first. I thought it was just for going to mass with him in the first place, since he hasn't been able to go much this year for lack of willing buddies, but he said it was something I did *at* mass. So probably the offering.

But it was *his* money I was giving. I was forcing *him* to be generous.

November 5
Kuala Lumpur, Malaysia

Big day tomorrow: graduation at the school. I was told to wear a black dress to accompany the choir, but I don't have one. So I'm borrowing Kori's skirt, and one of the women at the school sewed me my very own, very ugly shirt. It's a mustard yellow that looks horrific on my chronic sweaty sunburn.

It was a busy day for everyone, with graduation rehearsal and last-minute tasks, but when it was over, Tony suggested an "optional team hangout time" which of course ended up just being him and I.

It was a breath of fresh air. At the end of these days, I know we'll end up in the common room, talking until he gets sleepy.

I wish I could touch him but I can't because every touch is memorable. I can touch my whole team casually on the shoulder and hug them or elbow them or whatever, but him… it'd mean too much. I don't tap him on the head to get his attention or bump his knee under the table when something awkward happens at a meal or let our hands touch when I pass him a book in the library.

Kori and Robyn tease me: "Do you hold hands when you go to mass in the morning?"

No. Mass is important to him because he's Catholic. He hasn't had many chances to attend this year, so of course I'll be his buddy and help him go. That's bigger than my crush on him. So they can tease me all they want, but every day, I'll go with him.

Besides, if we held hands, the electricity would kill us.

November 7
Kuala Lumpur, Malaysia

I tried to watch *Muppet Treasure Island* with Tony. We watched thirty minutes before the internet failed. I could go either way on the Muppets and Tony thinks they're the shit. But he also loves the Jack Black version of *King Kong*.

Instead of watching stuff, we sat and talked about his family, and how he's so committed to the idea of having one. And how he'd rather spend money on his wife than himself.

We talked about fears. I said I was afraid of getting timid and not being myself at home and failing at theatre.

"But remember, you come alive when you're the underdog!" he said.

I gazed straight ahead and nodded and smiled. How did he know that? Who told him that? How did he figure that out?

We get along so well. I have a crush on Tony.

Tony said that talking with me is "Socratic." Does he even know what that word means? I don't.

November 9
Kuala Lumpur, Malaysia

We'll have our final debrief soon and that is basically when all the World Racers are allowed to start dating each other. I'm worried about it. Kori told me not to worry about it.

I get why we have the no-dating rule. Adding potentially romantic dynamics to an already intimate community is a recipe for trouble. But it's hard: it's not like 41 adults in their prime can turn off their feelings.

Anyway, it'll be over in a couple weeks and final debrief will happen and God willing, Tony and I will have a chat.

I am wracked with indecision. Some of the team and Vicki, Elisha's daughter, are going to Kuala Lumpur City Centre tonight to see a light show at the singing fountain by the Petronas Towers. I could go to that, or I could stay back and be with Tony, get reading done, learn, and probably watch a couple more minutes of *Muppet Treasure Island* before the WiFi stops working and we have another great talk. Tony doesn't want to go see the singing fountain. Too frivolous, maybe. I *can't* choose who to go with.

I know it's not a big choice but it matters a lot to me right now.

I went. I went with Arden, Kori, and Vicki. It was the right choice. Of course it was the right choice. How could I *not* sit on the steps beneath the Petronas Towers with hundreds of people and watch colorful fountains dance with the pop hits of yesterday? It was so fun. It was just water spraying in a mall plaza, but it made me feel alive, and *duh*, I should have gone, especially since there's so little time left here. Why did I even wonder?

Maybe Tony is not interested in spending the metro fare on such frivolities. I am. That's something good about me I should not tamp down. I am the kind of person who'd rather go out and see a singing fountain than stay home and flirt.

November 10
Kuala Lumpur, Malaysia

My favorite times of day here are the morning and the break after lunch. We eat, and I go across the hall to the quiet church sanctuary where it is air conditioned and dim and I read a book from Pastor Elisha's library. I'm borrowing G. K. Chesterton's biography of St. Francis now.

I haven't said anything about ministry, really.

I play piano for the choir, which is cool because I haven't played much this year but I'm not rusty at all. Arden and I are recording tracks with the four-part harmonies for their upcoming Christmas concert and we'll leave those with them. I play the soprano line, then the alto, then the tenor, then the bass. A song just came out called "All About that Bass" and Arden chants it when we get to that part of the songs.

There's painting. Just painting classrooms. There's always some other missionary's bad paint job to paint over.

Organizing the library. We make up our own categories. Tony and I have fun with it. Everything seems to fall into our "Inner Life" category.

Mass every morning.

Church on Sunday.

They give us food. Sometimes we go out and sometimes we eat at school: it's all fine, except for *nasi lemak*, which we often eat for breakfast. It comes wrapped in a banana leaf and it's spicy in a weird way. I think it'd be fine later in the day, but first thing in the morning, it's pretty awful.

We drink a lot of Milo, which is basically chocolate Nesquik. We order it hot or cold.

November 11
Kuala Lumpur, Malaysia
Two weeks left.

Every night now, Tony and I hang out, reading, talking, trying to watch *Muppet Treasure Island*. Of course, neither of us has said anything about our connection. But I'll be shocked if it doesn't come up in the next two weeks.

I can't see it working out but I still sort of feel like it should be gone through with. It's confusing. Like whatever's going to happen is going to happen and I don't want to halt it.

If *he* doesn't bring it up, what do I say? "Hi Tony, do you have feelings for me? Cause I don't know if I have feelings for you but I'm clearly obsessed with you."

November 13
Kuala Lumpur, Malaysia
This week I noticed a little thing on the back of my knee. It hurt so much, I couldn't sit with my leg bent. So I went to the doctor and he diagnosed me with my first staph infection.

The clinic was next door to our apartment. It had leather couches and a screen where they displayed the name of the next patient.

The doctor asked if I was with the group of Americans who were working at the school for the month, and I said yes. I showed him the spot on my leg and asked what it was. He pulled out a big yellow flashlight, shined it on my leg, and said something about pills and being fine by Saturday.

"Should I put this on it?" I asked, producing a tube of hydrocortisone cream I had picked up in Europe. He took the tube from me and stared at it blankly, puzzled at the Cyrillic letters.

"Where is this from?" he asked, cocking his head. It took me a second to decipher the question.

"Bulgaria," I replied. This seemed to confuse him more. He furrowed his brow and twisted his neck even more.

"What have you been doing?" he asked, with the amused, concerned tone of voice one might use on a child who has wandered too far from home.

That is a question I've fielded more times than I can count. It's always hard to answer adequately.

We are on an 11-month trip to 11 countries I never imagined I'd see. We burn trash and teach theology and get stuck between borders. We sleep in tents, attics, buses, and hostels. We eat what's in front of us. We're homesick but we're at home anywhere. This is our first/second/fourth/ninth month on the road.

Except this time, I said it was our last month.

"And everything has worked out with the passport and visas? You've been able to get into all the countries?"

"Well, for the most part. We had some problems in Africa."

"And what is your next country?"

All the other months, when people met us and asked where we would go next, we gave exotic answers like Mozambique or Cambodia and received impressed looks and cautionary tales of friends of friends who drank the tap water or were airlifted out with this or that disease. But now, our next country is the United States, and that elicits a different response.

People ask, "What will you eat first when you get home?" and "Are you excited to see your family?"

While I have answers to both those questions, and they are "nachos made with Doritos" and "yes," those also are questions I can't quite grasp yet because I am still here. In Malaysia. With things to do. I want to be a glorious dirtbag a little while longer.

When my time in America was almost over last December and I was getting ready to leave, life became more colorful. My departure always loomed, but I found myself appreciating little things more and more, whether they were the mossy trees in the back yard or long family dinners. The fact that so little time remained there made the place and the company that much sweeter.

I know time's running out on this trip because that same thing is happening here. Everything is feeling new again. You'd think it was my first month abroad, not my last. I've been reading street signs and appreciating their delightful inscrutability. The missing tile on the stairs to our fourth floor apartment has endeared itself to me, as have the elevator doors that close immediately after opening and have sandwiched every one of our team between them. I've been working with the choir for three hours a day, and it gets tiring to teach music for that long, but then I remember how special the time is, and then it's easy to love every minute. Don't get me started on my team, with whom I'd gladly spend every minute before we say goodbye. Even the heat makes me thankful, because it's one more thing about this place that reminds me that this time is special and this place is different.

When the doctor prescribed me antibiotics and sent me to the pharmacy window, it felt more like I was picking up another memorable souvenir than mere medicine. We left the clinic and made our way to the library we have been organizing, past the 7-11 with the cheap drinks, past the stray cats sleeping on motorcycles, past the KFC for deaf people, and past everything else in Sentul Raya that's come to feel like home for now until it's time to travel to the next country, which will be, finally, my own.

November 14
Kuala Lumpur, Malaysia

We were sitting on the couch last night and there was a moment where the conversation *had* to turn to "us." It was the most natural place for it to go. I felt it there so plainly, almost past the point of awkwardness or vulnerability. It was simply the next thing on the docket.

But then I remembered that talk had to be diverted, because it's not time yet.

I wonder about how compatible we actually are, but then I remember how I want to be open to possibilities. And I think I've had some sort of feelings for him pretty much since first meeting him. And I've never been in a serious relationship. I don't know how compatible you're supposed to feel before it starts.

Tony says "what not" a lot. Is that a problem or an adorable quirk?

November 15
Kuala Lumpur, Malaysia
The medicine for my infection hasn't been working. The school nurse looked at it and told me it was just flu medicine. So she threw it out and made a gauze pack of epsom salts. She taped it to my leg, and said that if I stay hydrated and change the dressing often, the salts will soak up the infection.

November 16
Kuala Lumpur, Malaysia
Tony had the team throw me a *birthday party*. My birthday is one month from today, but we won't be on the Race, so he talked to Mom to learn about what I like, and he hosted a Chelsea-themed quiz show, and there were balloons and cake.

He took a big piece of cake, but it fell into his lap, and he picked it up and ate it, but then cake was all over his face and clothes and hands and I snapped a picture and it's just the most joyful photo. He's tall and tan and traveled and wearing his nicest collared shirt, and he's covered in cake and he can't stop laughing.

November 17
Kuala Lumpur, Malaysia
Our team was sitting in a conference room at the school, waiting to get the day's ministry assignment. There was a whiteboard on the wall. Someone had written, in red, PERMENANT IS MEANS NON ERASABLE MARKET MEM UNDERSTAND!!!

I'd been wondering if catheter and cathedral were etymologically related, so I was looking up the words on my phone.

"I have something I need to share," I said. I took a long pause as I read the dictionary entries. The team went dead silent.

"Turns out that 'catheter' and 'cathedral' are *not* related to the same Greek word."

They all released groans and slapped the table.

"What the heck!"

"*Chelsea!*"

"We thought someone died!"

"Why were you so serious about that?"

"You kept looking at your phone frowning!"

"I thought something was wrong!"

We were on an escalator and towards the top, Tony turned around to tell me something, and then he stared at me for a long moment until he tripped on the floor at the end.

I can't take this. I just keep liking him more.

November 18
Kuala Lumpur, Malaysia
Today was the last day of ministry.

November 19
Kuala Lumpur, Malaysia
How do we do this? If he starts the talk, I tell him, "Yes, I have feelings for you. Yes, I've prayed about this. I want to talk about it with you."

And if he doesn't? I'll do it. I don't know how, but I'll do it.

Despite all I've experienced the past 11 months, this is a new thing. It scares me.

In the parking lot we saw a tiny black kitten hobbling along. And then a car ran over it. Tony and Arden tried to steer our eyes elsewhere but all of us girls freaked out.

Later, Tony's finger touched mine at the metro station and then I felt a lurch in my stomach. I don't know if he meant to. I don't know if it was because we saw that kitten get run over. It just felt different from all the other times we've touched. I didn't stop the contact for a long moment. It wasn't a big touch. If we didn't like each other, it would have gone unnoticed.

November 20
George Town, Malaysia

George Town is a delightful island full of backpackers, shabby architecture, and murals. We are staying at a hostel for a few days for our final debrief. Then we'll fly to America.

Tonight, a bunch of us went to see the new *Hunger Games* movie at a mall. I didn't have fun because Tony wasn't sitting next to me. He was in the row behind me.

Now I'm sitting upstairs in the common room at the hostel. I'm in a coin-operated massage chair, but I haven't inserted a coin.

I thought Tony might be up here, but he isn't.

Anyway, one of the leaders gave a talk to the whole squad about identity. Before the Race, I never thought much about identity. I wish I had, because it's simple: identity is who a person is. Anything that could be taken away from a person isn't his or her identity.

I often place my identity in the wrong things. I've put in a lot of time curating what I've deemed my identity. My whole life, pretty much everything I've done has been in the name of getting smart, pretty, talented, interesting, and popular. I've spent a lot of time practicing piano and reading my Bible and being valedictorian and plucking my eyebrows, not as a celebration of who I am, but as a fail-safe against rejection and obscurity.

But of course, my little card castle can tumble. It has this year. I've lived 11 months without any say in my work or location. For the first time in my life, I've lived for others (sometimes by choice, sometimes by force). I've done ministry I've sucked at. I've seen that no one's safety is guaranteed. I have taken little thought for my appearance. I have been away from my familiar world for so long, I forget what it means to strive for the conventional American Dream. I've left so much of what I've known, so much of what I once considered integral to who I am. Learning to leave places, to say leave people, to change plans, to give up expectations, to leave comfortable faith… it's made me more myself than ever. It has been a profound blessing.

I pray I don't forget that. I pray that if things get tough back home, if I lose my way or my health or my people, I will know in my bones that God loves me for my very existence, and that nothing can take that truth away.

Oh! *There's* Tony, coming up the stairs. I'm saying, "Hey, how's it going?"

He's saying, "Excellent," and he has no idea I'm writing about him as he walks around the room, checks his phone, and sits down in a chair not far from me.

November 21
George Town, Malaysia
Tony and I went looking for this old cathedral in George Town because he wanted a quiet place to do the liturgy of the hours.

"Would you like to come along?" he asked. "I need a buddy."

"Oh. Uh, sure. I guess I can."

So we walked and took our time and were lost a little, which is totally not his style. He likes mapping his routes and being efficient. But he knows I like to meander, so he didn't say exactly where the church was. He didn't say he was doing things my way, but it was obvious.

We found the place and did the liturgy and didn't go back right away.

The church was light and airy. Its domes were tastefully high and done up in shabby seafoam green.

Chintzy.

We walked around. Tony explained the Catholic paraphernalia for me and I translated all the Latin for him.

We sat back down in a pew and were talking about this and that. I talked about how it was hard to have conflict with Kori, how it was strange to be at the end of the trip, who was picking us up from the airport.

Eventually, we were just sitting there. I was looking straight ahead and he was looking at me. It felt like minutes passed in silence.

"So," I said into the quiet. "What about *this*?" I tapped his shoulder and mine and his shoulder and mine.

"You and me?" He looked surprised.

"Yeah."

"Oh. We're doing this now?"

"Yeah."

Pause.

"Okay," he said.

And finally we were looking at each other honestly.

He said he'd been planning to talk to me the last night of debrief. But we talked today and it felt *so good* to be honest about everything, finally.

He said he had feelings for me. He said a lot.

I told him that I wasn't sure, but over the last month, by spending so much time together, I realized I had feelings for him too.

Eventually, we had to head back for lunch. I didn't tell anyone anything back at the hostel, but Kori saw my flushed face and knew what had happened and it made her giddy.

In the afternoon, we walked far, wandering down the streets until we ended up at a coffee shop. We sat there and talked for a long time.

I told him my concerns and we talked through each one. We addressed how he is a staunch Catholic and I'm a staunch non-Catholic, how he wants to settle down and marry soon and I don't, how he lives in Minnesota and I live in Washington, how we value money differently. I told him that I was scared to be talking about all this.

"I've been single my whole life. I'm good at it. It's the most comfortable thing for me. So if this is going to be a thing, I want to take it slow."

"Me too. We need to take this slow."

So it sounds like these differences aren't deal breakers and we can work through them.

Plus, we're attracted to each other.

"You know how people have their own scents?" he said. "Well, sometimes, when we were working next to each other, I'd catch a whiff of you and get so distracted. It was nice."

I blushed and grinned.

"And... that's the creepiest thing you'll hear from me today."

Our feelings were on the table and our feet were under the table. Mine rested against his, and this time, I didn't shift away when I felt the buzzing.

And now we're walking around the hostel together and the squad is starting to catch wind of it. I feel almost ashamed. I'm worried people will think we're a bad couple. They know us both; they would know.

Arden gave me good advice: wait. Don't jump into a relationship now. Be separate and then see how you still feel. See if you miss each other when you go home. Figure out if it works out on paper. Then revisit it after the holidays.

That would be wise.

Realistically? Hell no, we're not waiting. There's no way.

I told Arden that I felt dumb for being the one to jump the gun and bring it up since Tony was going to bring it up anyway. He said not to worry about that. He asked if I felt at all embarrassed about my feelings. I said maybe a little, kind of.

Tony was in bed when I went to brush my teeth, and when I came back he came out of the other bathroom and said,

"Hey."

I paused and he walked toward me.

"I wanted to give you a hug goodnight."

And so with my dirty clothes in my left hand and toothbrush in my right, I slid into his arms with a loud inhale.

November 24
George Town, Malaysia

If I could talk to the Chelsea of one year ago, I'd say:

"Leave it all! Leave your home and your people. Leave your first squad, your route preferences, your team, your expectations. Do the scary things, because if you do, you will get more than you can imagine. You will win the Race and get the guy and circumnavigate God's earth doing it."

Tonight, C Squad had a big banquet. We all gave each other awards: Worst Beard, Best Singer, and so on. I won Best Blogger.

Then, Mateo and Jason walked me to the ugly little beach nearby—they didn't know quite where it was but I did because Tony and I were there yesterday—and they left me.

It appeared that a ceremony was about to start. There were candles stuck into the sand in a ring. Tony was standing in the water, wearing jeans and holding a bouquet of flowers and another candle.

I walked onto the beach and stood at the edge of the water.

"Hi," I said.

"Come join me," he said, extending his arm.

I was wearing pants too, but I went to him and he took my hand and we stood in the tepid, dirty Malacca Strait.

He gave me the flowers and held the candle and said a lot of nice stuff. He said he loved my intellect and beauty. He said he had been afraid other guys on the squad would try to pursue me before he had a chance. He had the broadest smile. I felt vulnerable, just standing there, letting this praise wash over me. I was cringing and grinning.

Eventually, we waded out of the ocean and sat on the beach in a glowing circle of candles. They were melting into the sand.

"Uh oh," he said. He pulled his team leader cell phone out of his pocket.

"Did it get wet?"

"Oh yeah." He pressed a few buttons. "It is ruined."

"That's not good."

"Good thing the Race is over."

Then, he produced what he had decided was "our" drink.

The Chelsea and Tony Official Love Cocktail is not wine, but a blend of black currant aloe vera juice and club soda in a wine glass borrowed from the restaurant next door.

I couldn't believe it was happening. Standing in the Indian Ocean with flowers and a man? Drinking chunky juice from a borrowed wine glass? Really?

What a surprise ending. Like the end of a movie.

November 25
The bus from George Town to Kuala Lumpur, Malaysia
It's 7:40 a.m. and I never expected it to end this way.

We drive through thick fog and forest and mountains. I have a big bouquet of flowers from the man sitting next to me. I've been blessed. My eyes are blessed to have seen what they've seen.

Kuala Lumpur, Malaysia
Tony's been calculating all the ways we can shuffle the squad around so we can sit next to each other on the flights. But we're seated alphabetically by last name, and Kelly is the only person between us.

So Kelly watched him for a while before she said, "Tony, what if I swap seats with you?"

Now, six-foot-four Tony will be sitting in the middle seat on two flights—he won't hear of me giving up my window seat—and couldn't be happier, and we're all laughing at him.

Leave It All

November 26
Los Angeles, California, United States
I can't ever sleep on planes, but Tony let me lean on him and I rested for hours and hours. He makes me feel so calm.

On the final descent into Los Angeles, my eye started to hurt.

It hurt worse and worse and by the time we touched down, I had a raging case of what I knew had to be pink eye.

Tony and I were holding hands when the plane touched down.

A lot of the squad left at the airport, but a few of us had a hotel booked for a couple days. The goodbyes were not as traumatic as I expected.

That night, Tony and I spent as much time as possible together, because he flew out in the morning. We walked all over the place, looking for a convenience store or some place with eye drops, but didn't find anything. Just hotels and parking lots and palm trees.

"Guess what?" he said. "We're walking in America."

We ended up sitting in the hotel lobby talking and planned to stay up all night since he hadn't paid for a room before his flight. But my eye was bad enough that I needed to sleep. He came into my room and, so as not to disturb Lacey, Rita, and Tara, lay by the door.

I brushed my teeth in the bathroom and ran a washcloth under cold water to put over my eye. I resolved to go to the doctor in the morning.

On the way out of the bathroom, I knelt down to tell him good-night and kissed his forehead in the dark.

Then he kissed me on the lips.

So I kissed him back.

How long was it? Not more than five minutes. When it was past the point of a quick peck, he straightened up and sat on his knees and I fell back on my heels and he held me tighter and I kissed him harder. I think his hand was on the back of my neck. I dropped the washcloth.

I was afraid Rita, Lacey, or Tara would wake up, so I kept pulling away and putting my thumb on his lips and looking over to their sleeping forms. But I kept coming back.

I didn't want it to end but then I did end it, abruptly.

"Night!" I whispered. I glided to bed and lay down and stared at the ceiling with my one good eye.

"You made me lose sleep," he said in the morning.

"Me too," I said.

We boarded the shuttle to the airport, so he could catch his flight to Minnesota.

"What was the deal with that?" he asked.

"You *kissed* me," I said.

"You kind of repositioned. I was heading for your forehead."

"You were not! And I wasn't trying to reposition!"

I guess that'll be the debate for years to come.

He said it wasn't what he'd planned. I feel bad for jumping the gun again. But we were both sure into it.

We came to the airport. We kissed each other several times on the lips, hard.

Then I boarded the shuttle and waved goodbye.

I took a long nap when I was back at the hotel. Then my other eye started getting bad so I went to a clinic with Lacey. I didn't have insurance, so it cost $145 for someone named Doctor Michael Scott to tell me that yes, I had pink eye.

I went to a CVS where everything was new and like, organic. The nail polish was very expensive. I didn't see any for less than three dollars.

I hope Tony doesn't get pink eye. He claims he won't but you can't just decide not to get pink eye.

November 28
The flight from Los Angeles, California to Seattle, Washington, United States

It's Friday and I'm writing the last page of my leather-bound journal.

"I've Had the Time of My Life" was playing when I boarded.

Leave It All

I'm in *America*. My family is here. It has been a week since Tony and I started dating.

Odds are I've contracted some tropical disease that'll take years to surface.

I'm scared of monotony.

When is the last time I had a bagel with cream cheese? Let alone one that cost three dollars. That's most of a day's food allowance.

I feel bigger and smaller than before. I feel like I've been put in context, and yet, or therefore, I occupy my space more.

The window is cold.

We are starting the final descent.

There's Seattle. I see a modest cluster of skyscrapers, hemmed in by dark mountains and the darker, labyrinthine Puget Sound.

And that's the end.

AFTER

One day after the World Race
Hours on long distance buses: 260. That's almost 11 days.

Hours on planes: 66.

Borders crossed: 23.

Countries I set foot in, not counting airports: 15. Honduras, Guatemala, El Salvador, Albania, Macedonia, Bulgaria, Kosovo, Italy, Zambia, Malawi, Mozambique, Thailand, Cambodia, Malaysia, United States

Currencies used: 12.

Most people fit in a 15-passenger van: 26.

Stamps in my passport before the Race: 6.

Stamps in my passport after the Race: 41.

My backpack's weight at the start: 38 pounds.

My backpack's weight now: 45 pounds.

Months I slept in my tent: 3.

Months I slept outside: 1.

Places I slept: 27.

Times I was miserably sick: 2.

Colors my hair has been: 3. Brown, red, and purple.

Dreadlocks: 1.

Sticks of deodorant lost: 3.

Hot showers: 60 or so.

Times I was electrocuted by a hot shower: 1.

Times I watched *King Kong*: 4.

Times I watched *How to Train Your Dragon*: 5.

Monkey movies (movies featuring monkeys in starring or supporting roles): 9.

Times I used a dishwasher: 3.

Times I walked more than a mile to get internet: lost count.

Times I ate rice: lost count.

Bowls of oatmeal: lost count.

New foods tried: lost count.

Sugar-free sodas consumed: 6.

Times I ate bugs on purpose: 2.

Times I ate bugs because I was too lazy to pick them out of my food: lost count.

Belongings lost, given, or stolen: lost count.

Double rainbows: 7.

Sermons I preached: 13.

Times I was offered a husband: 8.

Books I read: 17.

Times I washed my clothes in a machine: 25.

People I've been on a team with: 21.

Languages I've worshipped in: 12. English, Spanish, Farsi, Bulgarian, Bemba, Nyanja, Chichewa, Tombuka, Khmer, Bahasa, Tamil, and Burmese.

Wonders of the World we saw: 3. The Colosseum in Rome, Victoria Falls in Zambia, and Angkor Wat in Cambodia.

Days spent on the Race: 319.

Days left on the Race: 0.

Six days after the World Race
It's good to see everyone. It's cold. It's luxurious. It's funny how fast a pot of water boils. It's fun telling people that I have a boyfriend.

Two and a half weeks after the World Race
It's my birthday. I feel down. Depressed. As in, pressed down.

I'm never warm. I'm tired and I don't eat. I don't do dairy anymore. I'm sensitive to food all of a sudden. I'm scared I'll break Tony's heart.

There are good people here, but there's also a TV we always watch and shit we always buy.

In one way or another, the day revolves around buying shit. Unhappy? *Just go buy some shit.* It's the holidays. Time to buy shit for all the people in your life. Go put your makeup on and some trendy clothes so you can go to the mall and look good while you buy some shit and come home and wash it off and do it again tomorrow.

My time's not about serving and community anymore. It's about prosperity: pursuing it or languishing in it.

Three weeks after the World Race
I'm wrapping Christmas presents. The mumu I bought Mom in Malaysia looks cheap and I feel bad about it. There are ink stains on it. I can't wrap anything right. I'm afraid everyone will think I gave them stupid presents.

Two months after the World Race
A Catholic church in Everett flew Tony out from Minnesota for an interview to be a youth minister. They offered him the job. He wants to look pious so he said he would "discern what the Lord wants." But he's definitely going to take it so he can move here.

We talked about a lot of stuff. Found a place in Everett that does Central American food. Made out a lot. It feels fast for him to move out here, but it's good.

Dropping him off at the airport and walking back to my car in the garage alone felt really good. I almost felt more complete walking alone than I did with a boyfriend. I am so used to being by myself. I *like* being by myself. Yet, now I'm with someone. *Together* is becoming my norm.

Two and a half months after the Race
I should post a blog. I haven't written in two months. But what else is there to say? What I'm doing next? What God's doing next? My advice to Racers? I don't have anything to say.

One of the radical things about World Racers, they say, is their ability to leave behind all their worldly possessions and live simply and humbly. "Like the early Christians," I've heard. I suppose that's partly true. I did give up a lot of my comforts. It's a transition to sleep in a big room all to myself again, full of things I don't use and can't carry in my back all at once.

But I didn't really leave it all, did I?

I still had everything I needed *and* wanted on the Race. I had my laptop, iPhone, Nook, camera. I missed my thick blankets and fluffy pillows, but I had an expensive sleeping bag and sleeping pad that cushioned me from any real discomfort. Sure, my clothes were dingy. But I had a closet waiting for me at home and I had a credit card.

The thing is, as far as material possessions go, I didn't give up *that* much for the Race, and most people don't. I think we're kind of kidding ourselves to think we do...

I'm not going to post that.

Three months after the World Race

Today I've missed calls from my friends Jess, Courtney, and Caitlyn, and I need to call them back. I need to do work for tomorrow. All of this is fine and normal but I feel attacked and guilty for not having done it yet. I will, but I still feel guilty.

Another blog attempt I won't publish:

They tell World Racers to finish strong. I don't know if I did that. I got a crush on a boy and it hijacked the end of the trip. I told people I would keep blogging when I got home, but I haven't. I say it's good to be back and I'm excited for what's next, but I'm just confused.

But I owe my readers a proper update, I suppose.

Tony was offered a job at two Catholic churches in Everett. He bought a car and moved to Washington for me. I took a job teaching ESL at my old high school by virtue of there being no one else available and my having one month of experience in Cambodia. I'm also directing the school play and that sounds like a lame job, but it's not, because I love it.

But I do sit at home on the couch writing in my journal about Tony, and the dogs bark at me because I don't take them out on walks. I found what I want to do next, an apprenticeship in the music department of the prestigious 5th Avenue Theatre in Seattle, but I'm not qualified. Tony thinks I can do it but I don't know about it, and I also don't know about him.

I generally feel inadequate, and I'm comparing myself to people with real jobs. I feel like I'm wasting my education, and my privilege, and my year on the Race. I'm trying to be okay with being back. I'm trying to be okay...

Three and a half months after the World Race

How quickly the words fall out of my face: "Yes, I've been traveling. I did the World Race, a mission trip to 11 countries in 11 months. I lived in Central America, Eastern Europe, Southern Africa, and Southeast Asia."

"How was it?"

"Oh, it... was a lot!"

But people don't understand what "a lot" means, so then I say, "It was amazing!" Then they don't ask me anything else and I don't tell them.

A lot? Yes. Amazing? Yes. But more than anything, it's *over*.

I hate that it's over. I hate that I'm stuck in the beautiful house I grew up in. I want to go away. Can you believe I'm saying that already? I went all these places and dreamed of home, and now that I'm home with the plush carpet and potable water, I want to leave it all.

I frantically look on Workaway and WWOOF, consider paying the membership fees, and know it won't do any good today.

I remind myself that I have a *boyfriend*, and that's the best thing that can happen to a person. That's what every Christian dreams of getting from a mission trip.

Isn't it?

I eat broccoli with chopsticks and drink grapefruit juice and paint and watch the Marina Abramovic documentary because those are the most creative things I can think to do.

But it's not enough.

Four months after the World Race

I had a big life last year.

One year ago I was traveling from El Salvador to Bulgaria. I didn't like El Salvador, and things were better in Bulgaria, but there were still boring days, even "out there." The Race was epic, but it was boring once it became normal. I kept expecting my life to get big and epic but anyone can read what happened and see that I was already in it.

Which means I'm probably in it right now. But the familiarity of my life now is crippling and I wish I could leave it all again.

I try doing new things. I have a *boyfriend* and we're in love. I'm directing a high school play and teaching English. I've been going to yoga lately and I'm getting strong.

But last year I stayed fit by walking miles to grocery stores, not sweating in a suburban YMCA.

I wish I could write a blog and talk about this.

Four and a half months after the World Race

I'm waiting for Tony to get off work so we can spend the day together. I'm writing another blog I'll never post:

Once upon a time, a girl circumnavigated the world, got a boyfriend, and went back home.

Sometimes on Thursdays, she'd go to yoga at the Y, take a cold fast shower with no soap and the curtain partly open, and go to Michael's to buy yellow embroidery thread to weave around her dreadlock. She'd go to Starbucks, poop in the bathroom, buy a large iced coffee with cream but no sugar, and drive up 405 listening to audiobooks.

Her iPhone would direct her to a Catholic church, which made her feel both oppressed and strangely hip. She'd drive up there and think how cool she was for not wearing a drop of makeup, that her naked zits and dark circles and faint mustache were defiantly visible. How cool that her shirt was wrinkled and she'd cut off the sleeves herself and her hair was messy and her watch was scratched, and her lips were red and her Keds were white.

She'd drive 90 minutes to Everett and think about how cool she was, and how it was only a matter of time before she broke up with her boyfriend.

Five and a half months after the World Race
I finally published something.

Every time I get the urge to write this blog, I'm at a grocery store, dismayed that each food package has English on it.

I think about how it wasn't like that one year ago.

Then I get inspired: this will be the day I write about my reentry into my old life. I go home and open my laptop and write.

But then I don't know which things to say, because there could be so much to say. And then I think of other things I should be doing, and what I could say gets pushed aside.

I've been home for five and a half months. That's enough time to live in Honduras, Guatemala, El Salvador, Bulgaria, Albania, and Zambia, with time still to eat at Chili's in Houston and explore a castle in Kosovo. What do I have to show for *these* five and a half months?

I wanted to document my reentry process. I haven't.

Many people have asked me if I'd throw a party and show pictures and tell stories. I haven't.

Even more people have told me to compile my blogs into a book. I haven't.

I've just been wallowing in my new-old life. My feet are always clean. The carpet in my bedroom is squishy. I scoff at expensive church buildings. I miss my tent. I feel scornful of department stores. Most of my delicacy around the topic of bodily functions has deteriorated. I don't put ice in my drinks anymore. I lost my sweet tooth. I eat mushy fruit, bread with only a little mold, old soup, stale Cheetos.

I dream about the World Race. I dream of missionaries coming to my house. I put short wooden stools in the front yard and give them tea and sugarcane. I dream of flying over the Zambezi with Tony and planning our next free day.

Sometimes I get upset. I don't know why I get upset, but I forget that I was gone so long. I forget that I lived in so many places. I forget that what we all went through was not a dream. I forget that last year was so big.

So, what to do with all this?

Tony sent me a text that said, "It's been 150 days since the Race ended."

150 days will become a year, then two years, then five years. Time goes fast.

Something I am learning about reentry is that it's an *entry*, not just an exit. These 150 days and counting are not all about us coming back to America and crying in grocery stores. They are also about continuing forward. They are about opening my eyes to where I am. They are about being the person I became on the Race: a person who sees the people around her, no matter who they are, and loves the ground beneath her, wherever it is. They are about neglecting comfort zones and learning confusing things. They are about looking to the future but never ignoring the God-given days at hand.

The Race was just more of my life. It wasn't the pinnacle or the end. So even as I mourn its passing, I am trying to remember that more things will happen.

My sister asked if I was okay and if I wanted to hang out with her. I said I was busy with the application for the music apprenticeship in Seattle, and I didn't have time. And she said she was going to a friend's house but she'd stay home if I wanted her to. That almost made me cry. But I told her she could go.

Six months after the World Race
Last night I cried harder than I've cried in a long time. I cried on FaceTime at night while Tony drifted off to sleep even though I tried not to, and when we finally hung up so he could sleep more and I could cry more, I felt so alone.

I was so hungry. There was plain rice in the fridge and I took a handful and went upstairs and sat on my bed and ate it cold. I felt so much pain. I wondered if I'd ever buckle down and have a career. I wondered if I'd travel again. I especially wondered about this thing with Tony. I know we won't make it, but he believes we will. I wondered if that was enough. I keep fantasizing about breaking up, but I don't want another ending on top of everything else.

In desperation, I yanked open my nightstand drawer and grabbed the rose-scented rosary Nora gave me as a joke Christmas gift, "To match your Catholic boy toy." I gripped it as tight as I could, I don't know why. There's a little piece of skin pulled up on my palm: the only evidence that I was in agony last night.

I hated to push the doubts under the rug but I was tired. So I lay down and kept holding the rosary and willed God to show up and make things okay. I opened my Bible even though I didn't want to. I didn't even read it, I only opened it. I gripped the rosary and fell asleep.

I don't know how to deal with last year ending. I don't know how to leave this relationship. I don't know how to leave the encroaching normalcy of life. I feel fragile. I feel stuck.

Four years after the World Race
I came to hate what I wrote in Malaysia:

Leave it all! Leave your home and your people. Leave your first squad, your route preferences, your team, your expectations. Do the scary things, because if you do, you will get more than you can imagine. You will win the Race and get the guy and circumnavigate God's earth doing it.

But that was not the end. After being home from the Race for a year or two, I wished I had said something more like this:

No. Leave it all, and you'll end up with a man at the end of the Race, and you'll know it's not meant to be. You'll go to Vancouver for the Women's World Cup, and at a hostel, you will dump him. You will expect it to make you feel free, but it won't make you feel free. It will ruin you. You will feel ruined for a very long time—it will *embarrass* you how long you will feel ruined—and then you will move to Seattle and start a scary job in theatre and work yourself into the ground trying to just be mediocre. You will have major surgery for a scary tumor in your neck, and you will have no boy to hold your hand and tell you it will be okay. Your family will be getting sick and dying around you, and you will feel pummeled by diagnoses. You will be confused about what you're meant to do with your life, and you will try to pray, but you will suck at it, and you will be lonely.

But that was not the end either. Maybe this is closer to the truth:

Leave it all. You'll circumnavigate the globe and return to America with a boyfriend, a dreadlock, and a case of pink eye. You won't keep any of them.

You will not feel good when you come home. You will miss the person you were in 2014. You will leave the boy and be lonely. You will have surgery and be afraid. You will eat kale and do yoga to cope with feeling lost, but kale and yoga won't help. You will try to remember God, but very often, you won't.

After

You will move to Seattle and live in the city for the first time. You will meet many new people at church and work and pub trivia. You will be a musician in big, beautiful theatres, and a cashier in a Scandinavian deli. You will go on dates with nice guys. Your life will be different than it was on the Race, but it will not be smaller.

You will get antsy and energetic. You will start walking everywhere. You will walk hours and hours around Seattle. You will fear that the best season of your life has passed. You will fear that no adventure can top the World Race.

But do not worry. The day will come when you go to the San Juan Islands in the northwest corner of Washington. You will volunteer on a pig farm, and in your bedroom in the barn, you will begin to gather your World Race journals into one document. You will decide to write a… thing. You won't have the guts to say *book* at first.

You will fly to Spain and walk across the entire country as a pilgrim on the Camino de Santiago. By this time, your hair will be very long. Your dreadlock will be covered in beads, and the red dye you used back in Bulgaria will still shine in the sun. You will walk for six weeks straight in gut-wrenching celebration of what you have seen and known. You will celebrate all that happened before and during and after the Race: your questions, your inspiration, your travels, your friends, your grief, your past, your future.

You will sit on cliffs at the edge of Europe and watch the sun fall into the Atlantic. You will have a strong body and a big smile.

You will understand that you see only moments but God sees everything. You will realize that human stories are powerful not for their ratios of good to bad, but for their existence. You will understand that God is with you and you are not alone, and that knowledge will be more than enough.

Then you'll leave. You will fly back to Seattle. You'll cut your hair short and hide your dreadlock in people's shoes. You'll write a book. But that is not the end either.